REDBACK 3

DOG DAYS

AUSTRALIA AFTER THE BOOM

Ross Garnaut

Published by Redback,
an imprint of Schwartz Media Pty Ltd
37–39 Langridge Street
Collingwood VIC 3066 Australia
email: enquiries@blackincbooks.com
http://www.blackincbooks.com

Copyright © Ross Garnaut 2013
Reprinted 2013
Ross Garnaut asserts his right to be known as the author of this work.

ALL RIGHTS RESERVED.
No part of this publication may be reproduced, stored in a retrieval system, or transmitted in any form by any means electronic, mechanical, photocopying, recording or otherwise without the prior consent of the publishers.

The National Library of Australia Cataloguing-in-Publication entry:

Garnaut, Ross, author.

Dog days : Australia after the boom / Ross Garnaut.

ISBN: 9781863956222 (paperback)

Mineral industries--Australia--Economic aspects. Mineral industries--Government policy--Australia. Economic forecasting--Australia. Australia--Economic conditions--2001- Australia--Economic policy--2001-Australia--Foreign economic relations--21st century.

338.230994

Printed in Australia by Griffin Press.
The paper this book is printed on is certified against the Forest Stewardship Council® Standards. Griffin Press holds FSC chain of custody certification SGS-COC-005088.
FSC promotes environmentally responsible, socially beneficial and economically viable management of the world's forests.

CONTENTS

Introduction: Australia's Choice
1

PART 1

1. A World Transformed
21

2. The Reform Era
36

3. The Great Australian Complacency
60

4. The Hair of the Dog
81

PART 2

5. Reform for Full Employment and Stability
107

6. Reform to Raise Productivity
130

7. Population, Participation and Equity
154

8. The Public Sector and the Federation
169

9. Avoiding Dangerous Climate Change
192

PART 3

10. A Changed Political Culture
212

11. Public versus Private Interests
233

Conclusion
263

Acknowledgments
274

Notes
278

References
285

INTRODUCTION
AUSTRALIA'S CHOICE

It was December 2005, and Australians were enjoying the longest economic expansion – and the largest rise in incomes over a short period – that a developed country had ever known.

'There are Salad Days of economic policy,' I said to the annual dinner of the Economic Society in Canberra, 'days when the economy outpaces even people's expectations. These are the times when poor policy looks good enough, and ordinary policy looks celestial.'

It was the third year in which the China resources boom was massively boosting payments for Australian exports.

Yet the Salad Days would be followed by the Dog Days, I went on to say, 'days when celestial economic policy looks ordinary, and ordinary policy diabolical. It will be wise to save much of the economic fruits of the China boom, in case the extraordinary conditions that we are enjoying turn out to be temporary – as they always have in the past.'

The rest is history. Australians now have to make the best of the Dog Days.

This book places before Australians the fateful choice that we will make in the months and years ahead, about how to respond to harder times after more than two decades of extraordinary prosperity.

The Coalition's decisive 2013 election victory in the House of Representatives gives it the opportunity to take decisions in the public interest. If it uses this opportunity to occupy the centre ground in political life and govern with the welfare of the great majority of Australians in mind, it will at once conserve most of the gains in our standard of living of the past twenty-two years and entrench itself in power for a long period.

Alternatively, if it seeks to govern in the interests of its most powerful supporters, it will not be able to lead Australia away from rising unemployment, large falls in living standards, social tension and growing dissatisfaction with our institutions. Its lifespan is likely to be short. A new government will have to deal with the problems, and we cannot be sure at this distance that it would do better.

Neither major party took policies into the recent election that came to grips with the great challenges facing Australia. Both parties proposed policies that would in fact impede solutions.

The choice for the new Abbott government is between two radically different approaches. We can continue to conduct our public life as if the approaches that seemed

ADVANCE PRAISE FOR **DOG DAYS**

'This book is a must-read for anyone concerned with the economic and social future of Australia. Garnaut brings to the task one of our most penetrating economic minds in an astringent analysis of the challenges facing us. He presents a wide-ranging and detailed set of policies to meet those challenges successfully. The book is lucid, compelling and unburdened by political bias.'—BOB HAWKE

'Here is a brilliant guide to the future of the Australian economy that our prime minister, his Cabinet and indeed all members of parliament should study. We cannot be sure that big problems are ahead for Australia owing to the end of the China boom, but it is highly likely, and our government must be prepared. Ross Garnaut draws on the lessons of the past and an ability to explain complex economic issues. He has cogent things to say about our changed political culture.'—MAX CORDEN

'Ross Garnaut is the nation's most prophetic economist. Whereas economists are often criticised for not having seen problems coming, Garnaut is always focused on future risks. If you care about Australia's economic future, this book is a must-read. If you don't see a problem, it will set you straight. If you do, it will provide solutions.'—ROSS GITTINS

good enough in the Salad Days will still work in harder times. If this is our choice, we will continue to live behind the veil of ignorance that has descended over our public life during the past dozen years. We will make choices within a political culture that is distorted by the intrusion of market values into areas of public policy where they have a corrupting effect and produce poor results.

Or we can restore discipline of the kind that framed public choice in the reform era from 1983 to 2000, be prepared to think hard about policy rather than shout political slogans, and be guided by clear analysis even when it requires difficult decisions.

I call these the 'business as usual' and 'public interest' approaches to policy. They lead to radically different outcomes. If we continue with the former, we will live in greater comfort for a short while. But sooner rather than later we will experience deep economic recession with high unemployment – probably rising with recurring recessionary episodes without falling much in the years between.

The memory of 1974 to 1983 may help older Australians to imagine this future. In some ways the starting point is more difficult than it was in 1974, and the consequences of failing to deal with problems are worse. If we choose 'business as usual', we can expect disappointment as public services are diminished bit by bit in response to successive fiscal crises. We can expect bitter political conflict within our society, and unhappiness about our institutions.

Such tensions would be all the more dangerous because they would emerge at a time of international financial uncertainty, in a world dragged down by the overhang from the global financial crisis, and with the causes of that crisis mostly still at large. They would come at a time of ideological uncertainty, with doubts growing about whether the political and economic systems of the developed world still have the capacity to deliver prosperity to most of its citizens. They would be all the more dangerous because they would be emerging at a time of strategic uncertainty, when Australians' confident presumption that might is right and on our side is challenged by the rise of the Asian superpowers. And they would come at a time of the growing impact of climate change.

The public interest is the much harder choice, but it has better consequences. For Australia to choose this approach, many of us – enough to influence policy decisions at a high political level – will have to put aside the slogans that have replaced thought about public policy so far in the twenty-first century. We will have to reconsider propositions to which we have given unthinking assent. That's hard. Harder still, we will have to change our minds when the evidence supports change. The public interest approach will not be chosen unless many Australians are prepared to support policies that sometimes go against their immediate personal interests. Political leaders will have to introduce changes that disappoint their strongest supporters.

The odds favour the path that is easier for the immediate future. The odds favour Australians choosing 'business as usual' – what I have been calling, since 2004, the Great Australian Complacency of the early twenty-first century. But let us at least consider alternatives to sleepwalking into a deeply troubled future as if we had no choice at all.

This book seeks to explain the choice that Australia faces. It seeks to lay out the path to a better future in enough detail to show that there is indeed a coherent alternative to the Great Australian Complacency.

THE ECONOMIC PROBLEM THAT WE FACE

Part 1, Chapters 1 to 4, describes our economic problem and how it came upon us.

Between the 1990–91 recession and late 2013, when this book was going to print, Australia enjoyed the longest unbroken period of economic expansion of any developed country ever. During this time, average incomes, measured in international currency, rose from the lower middle ranks of the developed countries to, at their peak, 25 per cent higher than those of the United States and 50 per cent higher than those of the European Union – a status unknown since the great boom from the gold rushes of the 1850s to 1891 that incubated modern Australia.

The expansion of the 1990s was built on solid foundations: rapid increases in productivity. Yet the expansion of the decade that followed was built on sand that was bound eventually to shift: at first a housing and consumption boom funded by bank borrowing from international debt markets; and then an unprecedented lift in the 'terms of trade' (prices for exports relative to imports), leading to an increase in resources investment to an unprecedented share of the economy.

The housing and consumption boom ended by the mid-2000s. That would normally have disrupted the prosperity: the global financial crisis would have descended upon us at a time of weakness were it not for the timely arrival of the China resources boom.

This boom was caused by a historically unique period of economic growth in China: the strongest, longest episode of 'catch-up' growth that the world has ever seen, using energy and metals more intensively than other countries had done, which set the world's most populous country on the way to becoming the world's largest economy. It was a remarkable episode in history.

Through the second decade of this extraordinary expansion, Australian businesses and households became accustomed to easy increases in incomes, ever-lower taxation and rewards that bore no close relation to effort or achievement. They demanded more and more of these good things. Governments met those demands not through increased productivity, but with the bounties of the housing, consumption and resources booms. Incomes, spending and costs rose to heights that could be supported only temporarily.

The China resources boom has had three phases. The first, high terms of trade, started in 2003 and reached a peak in 2011. The second, investment, started before the Great Crash and paused through it, then gained strong momentum from early 2010 and reached a peak in 2013 before declining. The third, increases in export volumes, started strongly in 2012 and is likely to continue until about 2017. Since increased government revenues were mostly being spent as they arrived from 2003 (the surplus of about 1.5 per cent of Gross Domestic Product (GDP) was a small proportion of the increase in income), the first phase had much the largest impact on the national economy and the investment phase the second-largest, while the third phase will have the least impact. Adding the effects of the three phases together, the China boom reached its peak in late 2011, but was already contributing a high proportion of its eventual maximum impact by the time of the Great Crash of 2008. The impact of the resources boom on Australian economic activity declined from 2011 and is likely to fall rapidly from 2013.

Through the long boom our real expenditure and real incomes grew prodigiously. Australia's real exchange rate against all other countries – an inverse measure of our competitiveness – rose to unprecedented levels. This caused the stagnation and then decline of what had been vigorous exports of services and high-value manufactures.

The problem arose because we spent the benefits of the resources boom as they came in, as if it was going to be with us forever. That's a lesson for the future: next time we should save most of the increase in incomes generated by any resources boom that might come our way. But it's too late after the peak of the boom to do that now. The result is that we are internationally competitive in too few activities to maintain full employment without running into external payments problems, unless we greatly improve our competitiveness.

The dog is barking. The fall in prices for resources from their 2011 peak is bringing down federal and state government revenues. Investment in resources has reached its peak and is about to go into decline. The volume of resources exports is increasing rapidly, but they do not have enough domestic impact to maintain full employment. Nothing else is growing strongly to replace the contribution of the resources sector. On current trends, we are headed for lower average incomes and employment.

HOW WE GET OUT OF THE PROBLEM

Part 2, Chapters 5 to 9, describes what we can do to maintain full employment and as much as possible of our living standards.

The first thing is to become much more internationally competitive. The only way that we can bridge the huge gap in costs between us and our international competitors is through a large fall in the real value of our dollar. By real, I mean a fall that does not lead to compensating increases in local incomes and costs as import prices rise.

How do we lower the dollar? There is scope to lower interest rates further. That makes capital inflow into Australia less attractive and pushes down the dollar. If that alone does not do enough because other developed countries are artificially lowering their own currencies, we can look at other measures. While there is still scope for lowering interest rates, we should make sure that this and not increasing government expenditure is the main way that we boost economic activity, because it is the combination of tighter budgets and looser money that takes the dollar down.

It is not easy to turn a fall in the dollar into a real depreciation of the currency and therefore into an improvement of competitiveness. As the dollar falls, Australian incomes are squeezed by the higher prices for imports (shirts, shoes, petrol, cars, iPads and holidays in Bali) and exportable goods and services (meat, dairy products and hotel rooms in Cairns).

Some may ask: why not simply boost economic activity and employment by increasing government spending, as we did in response to the global financial crisis, and by cutting taxes and reducing interest rates to promote private spending?

We could do that for a while, building up government and private overseas debt that will then have to be paid for by Australians who come after us, who may not be in a better position than we are to manage it. But not enough to avoid a big slump and not for long if we care about the future. Our external position is weaker now, after the China boom, than it was following the global financial crisis. Certainly, we are experiencing strong growth in resource exports, but our low competitiveness has stopped the growth of other exports. And each dollar of resource exports contributes less to domestic incomes and economic activity than the average dollar of other exports.

If we only increase spending at home, a large excess of foreign payments over earnings will emerge. We will soon find it difficult to obtain enough overseas money on reasonable terms to cover the excess.

The only way around this is through a large increase in exports from our services, manufacturing and agricultural industries, at the same time as we get as much value as possible from resources exports. That has to be preceded by large increases in investment in these industries. Such new investment requires a reversal of the decline in Australia's international competitiveness over the past decade. It requires a big fall in the real exchange rate – probably by 20 to 40 per cent from the giddy heights of the first quarter of 2013.

In early 2013 I became more and more concerned that the Great Australian Complacency had extended to nonchalant acceptance of the immense and immensely damaging overvaluation of the Australian dollar. The prime minister, other senior ministers, senior officers of the Reserve Bank and leading commentators all advised businesses and the wider community that they would just have to live with the strong dollar, and that what did not kill them would make them stronger.

There were several problems with the conventional wisdom. There was a risk that the dead firms would be more numerous than those strengthened by an uncompetitive exchange rate. The end of high prices for minerals and energy and of new resources investment was approaching rapidly, but without any sign of strong growth in other export industries. And it was not true that Australians simply had to accept without complaint a dangerously overvalued exchange rate: other countries had taken action, and we could too.

In February, I came to the view that unless the value of the dollar fell, it would condemn Australians to a recession that would be as unnecessary as, and more damaging than, the one in 1990–91. I embarked upon a series of public seminars and lectures in Melbourne, Canberra and Beijing. I also held private meetings with senior Australian economic officials.

After a big fall in the real exchange rate, it will take time for the non-resources export industries to gather strength and grow again. There will be no economic response until this fall has been with us long enough to convince business leaders that it is here to stay. You cannot fatten the pig on market day.

A big fall in the exchange rate doesn't sound so difficult. It started to happen in May 2013, with the Reserve Bank's cut in interest rates and change of rhetoric on the strong dollar, and it will continue as operators in the international money markets recognise the weaknesses in Australia's external position with the approaching end of the China boom.

Unfortunately, the dollar's fall is just the beginning of the adjustment that Australians must make at the end of the long boom. What matters is not the exchange rate that is displayed on the television news each night, but the real exchange rate – the overall competitive position of Australia after taking into account differences in inflation rates and productivity growth. A fall in the exchange rate would raise average prices. This would reduce living standards – the amount of goods and services that can be afforded – unless there are corresponding increases in the productivity with which Australian resources are used.

No doubt there would be pressure on government to negate the effects of a falling dollar by allowing incomes and spending to increase to match the rising price of imports. But if everyone is protected from the rise in import prices, no one is protected: the fall in the exchange rate gives us inflation and no improvement in competitiveness, and the old problems return exactly as they were.

Australia enjoyed growth in total productivity of 2.5 per cent per annum in the 1990s. That is as good as it gets (productivity growth has natural speed limits). It is unrealistic to think that having higher productivity growth than the rest of the world will by itself do enough to improve our competitiveness over the next few years. But higher productivity can help: the greater the improvement, the less the required cut in real incomes and expenditures. In addition, the more steps taken now to improve productivity in future (and most reforms yield their fruits only after many years), the less risky it will be to increase foreign debt to fund partial maintenance of incomes during the adjustment period.

By how much do real incomes and expenditures need to fall as productivity rises? If there is a large drop in the exchange rate and a corresponding revival of investment and exports, the fall in incomes and spending only has to be large enough to make up the gap left by the decline in the terms of trade. Not small, but not frighteningly large. We will come back to the numbers later in the book.

If we do not shift our production towards exports and our spending away from imports, and the whole of the adjustment is instead achieved by cutting spending, then the fall in living standards will be very large for many Australians. This will happen automatically if we choose 'business as usual'. The adjustment will be forced on us by international financial markets as they gradually realise that we are at the end of the China boom, and as the unusually expansive monetary policy of the big developed countries returns to normal. Worse, it is likely that the fall will be unevenly spread, with a disproportionate burden being carried by the rapidly growing number of Australians who want paid work but can't find it no matter how hard they look.

So this is the economic choice. Do we accept persistent large increases in unemployment and large declines in living standards under 'business as usual'? Or do we accept a public interest approach: think hard about how to achieve a large reduction in the real exchange rate, lift productivity and share a moderate reduction in living standards across the community?

If we choose the latter approach, we can reach real depreciation in more or less equitable ways. The difference is large in relation to ordinary Australians' standard of living. The political reality is that if we do not make the adjustment fairly, it will be hard to do it at all.

If we choose public interest reform, we are also choosing to make large changes to some recently but deeply entrenched features of our political culture. That is the hard part of the choice.

CAN OUR POLITICAL SYSTEM MANAGE GOOD POLICY ANYMORE?

Part 3, Chapters 10 and 11, analyses the deterioration in our political culture so far this century, which makes the job of a government seeking to manage in the public interest much harder.

Many changes are necessary for Australia to choose the public interest approach. Every one of them involves some loss of income for some people, and some sacrifice of short-term comfort for future gain. Viewed in isolation, each element of reform is politically challenging. Viewed together, at first sight they look impossible.

A paradox of reform is that it is sometimes easier to make many changes all together rather than one by one, even though each of them is difficult politically. Households and groups may recognise that they will benefit from the reform programme as a whole, although they are hurt by some elements of it in isolation.

Whether comprehensive public interest reform is possible depends a great deal on the quality of political leadership. Quality of leadership is partly about the confidence a society has in its leaders. This is the elusive quality of prime ministerial popularity that was important to the success of the Lyons government in managing measures that gradually took us out of the Great Depression, and to the success of the Hawke government in its reforms of the 1980s through to 1991.

Quality of leadership is partly about a capacity to explain the nature of the choices that must be made on our behalf. Public education is an essential element in any reform programme. It was critical to the productivity-raising reforms, especially of the Hawke government, and also under prime ministers Paul Keating and, in his early years, John Howard.

Whether comprehensive public interest reform is possible also depends a great deal on whether there is a substantial independent centre of the national polity. By an independent centre, I mean those people and groups who take an interest in issues affecting national economic performance and assess each policy by its effects on the Australian public interest and not by its effects on their personal or corporate interests or the fortunes of the political parties with which they are aligned. Participants in the independent centre publish the results of their work without constraint. The independent centre includes not only private elements, but also public ones with traditions and rules that support independence. In Australia these include the core agencies of government, such as the Treasury and Finance departments and the Reserve Bank. The Productivity Commission has played a big role both as part of the centre and as a contributor of information and analysis to strengthen the participation of others in policy development. The universities and their associated think-tanks have traditions of independent contributions. So do other research institutions established with funding arrangements, constitutions and traditions that ensure the people within them can undertake work and publish conclusions that are not determined by private or partisan interests. The centre also includes the best of the media.

Of course, the ideal of independence is not always perfectly realised. The contributors to the Australian independent centre are human. But there is always potential for its mobilisation within the Australian polity.

Economic reform in the public interest is difficult anywhere and anytime. It is more difficult in a democratic polity, where citizens tend to judge harshly leaders who ask for sacrifice of some private comfort for the public interest, or some current comfort for future benefits.

National difficulties or even full-blown crises do not automatically transform this reality, as demonstrated by the fate of European governments in the aftermath of the Great Crash of 2008. Difficulties and crises do, however, provide opportunities for the exercise of high orders of leadership, if the people in office at a time of crisis are up to the task and have before them well-judged programmes of reform.

It is an unhappy reality that policy change in the public interest seems to have become more difficult over time, at least in the capitalist democracies, and probably in authoritarian market economies like China as well, as interest groups have become increasingly active and sophisticated. Two things have changed. First, the range of instruments available for influencing policy has expanded with the modern media, and this has transformed the way that the old media presents public policy choices.

The second change reflects a social shift. Scholars of politics, sociology and economics have long observed that a successful market economy requires citizens to accept restraint in the pursuit of private interest outside the sphere of the market. Capitalism doesn't work if all of us seek to maximise our private interests in every interaction with society. Leaders will take payments for delivering policies that favour one group over another. Executives will take risks with the assets of public companies in the course of making decisions that increase the value of their own share options and rights; workers will hold their enterprises to ransom; judges will extract personal benefits from their decisions. The law cannot operate if everyone pushes it to the limit for their own advantage. Yet this is how markets do work in many countries – and why markets don't work in those countries.

The economist Fred Hirsch said that capitalism works because it stands on the shoulders of a pre-capitalist (religious) ideology, and that the waning of this moral legacy over time is a threat. Groups of many kinds have come to feel less inhibited about campaigning overtly for their private interest against government's assertions that measures are in the public interest.

Modern economic life everywhere is testing how far private interests can set the rules for a market economy. This is making reform in the public interest more and more difficult, and explains the challenges that US and European governments have had in managing the aftermath of the Great Crash. Chapter 11 discusses an important manifestation of this phenomenon in Australia: private interests' commitment of large sums of money to interventions against specific government proposals.

The challenges are more acute in Australia following the boom. For a long time, no private interests of any kind were asked to accept losses in the cause of improved national economic performance. A new ethos developed within the Great Australian Complacency, which held that there can be no losers from reform. Businesses demand compensation for correction to errors in policy from which they are drawing profits. Households have been led to expect that no change will cause any of them to be worse off. But compensation for any negative effect of a change in policy can cancel out much of the benefit of reform. It is a step forward that some households were moderately disappointed by the budgets of 2012 and 2013.

These are all reasons to be doubtful that our society will choose a public interest response to the problems that lie ahead. The later chapters of this book discuss the policies that would be part of such a response, as well as the political challenges that would have to be met. They seek to discuss realistically the difficulties facing reform. And they consider some reasons for hope that Australians may yet choose the public interest approach.

I also examine critically some of the recent episodes of unconstrained private pressure on the policy process. For example, a closer look leads me to question the received wisdom that the campaign against the mining tax in 2010 was effective in winning over public opinion. It was certainly effective in obtaining a policy outcome, but a cool look at the data informs us that the campaign did not persuade the public. Later chapters also take a close look at what made far-reaching change possible in the face of intense pressure from private interests in the reform period of 1983 to 2000.

Dog Days concludes that we do have a choice. An Australian leadership committed to the public interest approach, supported by a substantial community of concerned and engaged Australians, could achieve the better outcome for the nation.

The scale of what is at stake makes it worthwhile to try.

PART 1

CHAPTER 1
A WORLD TRANSFORMED

Australia must find its way in the Asian Century, at a time when the global balance of economic power is shifting. But this is nothing new: Australia's economic fate has always been shaped by developments in the wider world. In what follows I trace the story of the modern global economy from its inception to the present. I return to Australia in Chapter 2.

It was the participation of China in modern economic growth from 1978, and then the pace and structure of Chinese development through the early years of this century, that gave us our resources boom. It is China's shift to a new phase of economic growth, as well as the usual global supply response to high commodity prices, that has brought the boom to an end. Nevertheless, as they continue to grow, the large Asian countries, led by China, India and Indonesia, are set to generate more diverse opportunities for Australia in the twenty-first century.

MODERN ECONOMIC GROWTH IS FULL OF SURPRISES

Modern economic growth originated on the island of Britain only 250 years ago. Today it is still young, raw and changing rapidly. It creates new challenges for humanity as it changes. Right now we are working out as we go along how to reconcile economic growth with the natural and sociopolitical conditions that maintain our civilisation.

While modern economic growth emerged first in Britain, it was the creation of the whole of humanity. It built upon the advances in science and technology that had been gathering pace since the Mongol conquest brought the technological knowledge of Sung Dynasty China to the rest of Eurasia, and since interaction with the scholarly wisdom of Islamic Spain introduced Christian Europe to the mathematical genius of India and the Arab world, and reintroduced it to the intellectual achievements of Ancient Greece. It built upon the innovations in government over large-scale concentrations of people that emerged out of what are now Iraq, Iran and North Africa; the valleys of the great rivers flowing from the Himalayas through the Indian sub-continent and China; and the Roman Empire, along with the smaller states that succeeded it in the Middle East and Europe. And it built upon the systematic questioning of established religious beliefs and practices by the Germanic communities of central Europe.

Over its first century, the new economic growth took root in Britain's overseas offshoots, including Australia, in adjacent areas of Europe and then in the islands of Japan. It involved the accumulation of capital and the acceleration of invention, which was then applied to commercial processes in order to raise the rate of growth in output.

In the first thousand years after the birth of Christ, the world's economic output increased by only one-sixth, entirely contributed by population growth. By contrast, in the second millennium, as the late Angus Maddison's careful work tells us, global output increased 300-fold. In this time, the world's population increased twenty-two times and output per person thirteen-fold. The expansion in the second millennium mainly occurred after the Napoleonic wars, as the industrial revolution spread through Europe.

Modern economic growth greatly enhances the power of those states in which it takes root. It underwrote imperialism, through which a small part of humanity came to control the lives of almost the whole of the rest. At first it conferred wealth and power mainly on a small number of people in what were becoming the advanced economies; but as it continued over long periods, it came to be associated with rising wages and a broad increase in standards of living. At this stage, it elevated the knowledge, health, longevity and mobility of ordinary people above those of the elites of antiquity.

Modern economic growth fuelled the international exchange of goods, services, capital and technology. It also accelerated the global movement of people, which has been part of the story of human development from the time we left Africa sixty or seventy thousand years ago.

Imperialism extended the spread of economic exchange. However, it did not introduce modern economic growth to the mass of people in South Asia (the British Empire in India extending over what is now Bangladesh and Pakistan), China, the densely populated regions of Southeast Asia and the diverse territories of the Ottoman Empire.

The youth of modern economic growth and our inexperience with it mean that it frequently surprises us. Each new cycle and episode of structural change, each new institutional and technological development, and the accompanying changes in beliefs and institutions and practices, poses dangers to the natural world as well as to the institutional foundations of growth itself. It is never certain that each new problem will have a solution. We discover our destination when we get there.

CATCHING UP IS PAINFUL BUT REWARDING

The high-income economies are at the frontier of change. They grow through the invention of new ways of doing things that alter the economic, and in turn the social and political, structure of our lives.

We now know that once a number of essential conditions have been met, people from any cultural background can partake of modern economic growth. We also know that growth can proceed more rapidly for newcomers, while they are catching up, than for established economies. The newcomers do not have to invent the technology and institutions for themselves; they can absorb these quickly from the international economy.

But such societies must have made growth their priority. They must have effective states, which ensure the provision of a range of public goods and establish a reasonably open exchange of goods, services, technology and capital with the international economy. The new entrants to economic growth can also absorb capital from developed countries, and use their relative abundance of natural resources and labour to generate large gains from trade.

Yet for the latecomers, modern economic growth is more than catching up. It disrupts established beliefs, relationships and ways of organisation. It only takes root where the view is widely held that it is worth the cost. Otherwise, many old and new centres of political power find ways of frustrating its progress and sabotaging the reforms that are necessary to sustain it. Even when there is broad agreement on priorities, old institutions have to adapt to new circumstances, resulting in the emergence of hybrids.

It should therefore be no surprise that most developing countries at first viewed modern economic growth with caution in the aftermath of the collapse of imperialism following World War II. It was the failure of the alternatives, and the prosperity and power of those countries that experienced economic expansion over long periods, that gradually caused developing countries to seek deep integration with the international economy.

Speed limits are imposed by the quality of policy-making within government; the effectiveness of institutions, business leadership and organisation; the education and training of the workforce; and the capacity of all to accept and manage change.

Several East Asian economies were pioneers of modern economic growth in the post-war period: Hong Kong, Taiwan, Singapore and South Korea. Their success was influential in other countries, at first especially in Southeast Asia – most decisively Malaysia and Thailand.

The impact of modern economic growth increased immensely when it put down roots in the three most populous of the world's developing economies. The shift crystallised in China in 1978, Indonesia in 1985 and India in 1991. There was a much stronger reliance on markets and a deeper integration with the international economy. This led over time to a shift in the centre of gravity of the global economy towards Asia – a development that set the scene for the Asian Century.

Since 1978, China has experienced consistently rapid economic expansion, for longer and more strongly than any country in history.

India's inward-looking policies in the early decades after Independence generated growth rates around 3–4 per cent. Market-oriented reform with greater integration into international markets saw this rate double in the two decades after 1991.

Indonesia, the third-most populous of the developing countries, has experienced even stronger growth than India, thanks to its adoption of outward-looking policies in the late 1960s and then again in the mid-1980s. Indonesia, like much of Southeast Asia, grew especially rapidly in the 1990s, until the Asian Financial Crisis of 1997–98 provided a lesson about speed limits. The catastrophic decline of output in 1998 destroyed the authoritarian Soeharto government and led to a swift and remarkably smooth transition to representative democracy. The new political foundations were sound enough for Indonesia, like China and India, to experience only a modest downturn after the Great Crash.

DEVELOPING COUNTRIES GROW FASTER IN THE TWENTY-FIRST CENTURY

The big Asian countries were the largest part of a more general shift. The elites of more and more countries came to view the pain and disruption of sustained rapid growth as preferable to the poverty and strategic weakness that accompany the alternatives. Developing countries generally – most powerfully in the rest of Asia and most surprisingly in Africa – experienced higher rates of growth in the early twenty-first century and maintained much of their momentum despite the aftermath of the Great Crash of 2008.

I call this period of widening participation in rapid economic growth the Platinum Age, following what economists came to call the Golden Age of the immediate post-war decades.

Before the Great Crash it seemed that the Platinum Age was also to be enjoyed by the developed countries, helped by the availability of cheap capital from the savings of China and the resource-rich developing economies. There were also expanded opportunities for trade with Asia. Australia and other suppliers of energy and metals experienced a large increase in their terms of trade. Suppliers of capital goods for which there was Chinese demand were also well placed, Germany and Japan most of all.

For reasons that we do not yet understand fully, productivity growth slumped in the developed countries from the beginning of the twenty-first century. For a while, the effects of this decline were obscured by a debt-funded housing and consumption boom. Extremes of financial deregulation and a lack of prudence and morality contributed to a historic lift in asset prices and consumption.

THE GREAT CRASH SLOWS THE DEVELOPED WORLD

From 2007, the flaws in banking were revealed in the failure of one financial institution after another in the United

States and Britain, and then on the mainland of Europe. The collapse of one of the largest American banks, Lehman Brothers, in September 2008, precipitated a general disintegration of confidence in financial institutions. Banks would not lend to one another. For a while in late 2008 and early 2009, international trade shrunk more rapidly than in the early stages of the 1930s Great Depression. This was the Great Crash of 2008.

In contrast to what happened after the Great Crash of 1929, governments and their central banks moved quickly. They guaranteed the massive debts of large private institutions and provided them with cash. They reduced interest rates and loosened budgets. Heads of government attended meetings of the G20 group of major economies in an effort to build support for concerted action. The scale and speed of the implementation of anti-recessionary policies was greatest in the Western Pacific, with China's response being crucial to the containment of the downward spiral, and then to the recovery of regional and global economies.

In some countries – notably Spain – recession turned a sound public fiscal position into a catastrophically weak one. In a number of countries, concern about public debt led to policies of austerity, leading to another slump in activity and even higher budget deficits. The US Federal Reserve, the Bank of England, later and less enthusiastically the European Central Bank, and later still but more enthusiastically the Bank of Japan stimulated their economies through an unprecedented purchase of private assets with cash created for the purpose.

The Great Crash of 2008 ended the artificial boom and left the developed world to live with the reality of low productivity growth. Conditions were made more difficult in many countries by an overhang of public and private debt from the Crash. In the Eurozone, the crisis laid bare unresolved problems of managing a common currency area without a common budgetary system.

Beyond the crucially important possibility of an increase in employment, there is no prospect in the foreseeable future of average living standards rising in the developed countries of the North Atlantic. Indeed, a focus on the average obscures declining living standards for large numbers of people. In the United States, for example, high incomes have risen strongly through this period, while those of ordinary citizens have fallen.

This tendency in most of the developed world has its origins partly in structural features of contemporary economic growth, and partly in changes to regulation and taxation. Jeffrey Sachs and the Nobel laureates Joseph Stiglitz and Paul Krugman are among US economists with high reputations who attribute the latter changes to the increased influence of money in the democratic process.

The rising living standards of ordinary people in developed countries in the decades after World War II supported the legitimacy of capitalism and liberal democracy in competition with communism. Now, if living standards for ordinary people continue to fall, this will have large and unpredictable ideological and political effects.

The large developing countries were affected much less by the Great Crash of 2008. The financial crisis therefore was an inflexion point, after which the relative shift in economic and strategic weight towards the developing countries accelerated and became more obvious to everyone.

China is the biggest story in this historic shift in the centre of gravity of the world economy and will remain so for years to come. It was the largest contributor to absolute growth in the volume of world output and trade from the turn of the century to the Great Crash, and overwhelmingly so from 2008. Its role in the growth of world savings available for investment was proportionately even greater.

ECONOMIC GROWTH IN CHINA IS CHANGING

Understanding the nature of China's economic development is essential to understanding the contemporary world. This development falls into three periods. From 1978 to 1984, reform was concentrated on agriculture and rural development. A rapid increase in rural living standards established a political base for the wider and deeper reforms that followed.

From 1984, the focus shifted to urban and industrial expansion, with a rapidly deepening interaction with the global economy. China entered a period of uninhibited expansion in investment that continued until 2011. This had three sub-plots. Until 1992, there was uncertainty about the boundaries of political and economic reform, and changes in policy were part of a search for an ideological basis to support a deepening use of markets, private ownership and integration with the international economy. From 1992 until late in the decade, there was a tighter drawing of political boundaries alongside rapid liberalisation of trade and payments, a greater use of markets to set prices, and more private ownership.

The deepening integration with the international economy was entrenched by China's acceptance into the World Trade Organization in 2001. However, the movement towards markets and private ownership stalled with the colossal expansions of state-related expenditure following the Asian Financial Crisis of 1997–98 and the Great Crash of 2008. In response to these two external recessionary threats, large state-owned and state-connected enterprises invested massively in heavy industry, infrastructure and urban development. The Chinese economy under the Communist Party had always been associated with an exceptional intensity of metals and energy use; this was reinforced by the new pattern.

This period of rapid, investment-led growth was challenged by its own success from 2004, with a growing scarcity of labour and rapidly rising wages. The new conditions made their first appearance in coastal cities and have been present in most rural and urban areas in recent years. They have been reinforced by deliberate policy steps to counter growing inequality, increase the share of consumption and services in the economy, and deal with environmental problems. The new Chinese economic model will involve moderately lower rates of growth (averaging 7–8 rather than 10 per cent), and markedly less energy- and metals-intensive growth, together with less dependence on coal as an energy source.

While China was growing rapidly in the old model, its high savings kept the global cost of capital low, despite excessive spending in the English-speaking countries and Spain. China's new model involves lower savings and will cause global interest rates to be substantially higher than they would otherwise have been during any return to growth in the developed countries. This will slow global recovery.

When China's exports were concentrated in simple, labour-intensive goods, the prices of these fell on world markets. Now that its specialisation is shifting to more complex and capital-intensive products, the prices of simple manufactured goods will rise – textiles, clothing, footwear, toys and the low end of electronics.

On the import side, China accounted for more than three-quarters of the growth in world demand for steel in the early years of this century, and over 90 per cent from 2005 to 2010. In the most recent period, which straddles the global financial crisis, China contributed over 80 per cent of the increase in global demand for petroleum, just over 100 per cent of this for aluminium, nearly 150 per cent for nickel and over 200 per cent for copper.

The vastly increased demand took suppliers of these commodities by surprise. There was little investment in expanding old mines and developing new ones to meet the requirements of China. Prices for iron ore, thermal and steel-making coal and some other metallic minerals rose to unprecedented heights between 2003 and 2008, fell back briefly in the months after the Great Crash, and then rose to new record levels in 2010 and 2011. For commodities, China's massive monetary and fiscal expansion, disproportionately focused on activities that raised demand for metals and energy, outweighed the stagnation in other major economies.

That all changed with China's new model of economic growth. The changes were discussed and tentatively introduced before the Great Crash. They were embodied in the twelfth Five-Year Plan (2011–15), and their effects began to show up in the economic data from 2012.

China's adjustment to this new model marks a hinge point in world history: the moment after the economic balance has shifted between the developed and developing countries. Today, developed countries are struggling with low productivity growth and growing inequality. Developing countries are mostly catching up at a historically rapid rate – although the big ones have faced new headwinds in 2013. The developing countries, by virtue of their rapid growth, are adding to pressures on the natural environment. Their entry into economic modernity raises any number of political and social challenges.

For Australia it is time to think about life after the boom, and the lessons that can be learned from the resource rushes of the past.

CHAPTER 2
THE REFORM ERA

In the second half of the nineteenth century, Australians enjoyed by far the world's highest material standard of living for ordinary people. A rich endowment of natural resources was turned into gold, wool and other commodities for sale to industrialising Europe, supported by institutions, policies and social structures that rounded out a dynamic advanced economy.

Scarce labour and high incomes meant many features of modern liberal democracies made their first or early appearances in Australia: compulsory school education and widespread literacy; large-scale use of public libraries; a self-confident workforce; organised sport as mass entertainment; and a democratic franchise. The reasonably equitable distribution of wealth and income, and access to education, helped to preserve democratic institutions when they collapsed in times of crisis in other nations that owed their prosperity to natural resources.

Our average incomes relative to those of other developed countries fell steadily through most of the twentieth century to below the global average, although they made up some ground during the 1990s. Then, in the early twenty-first century, average Australian incomes in international currency rose rapidly until they surpassed those in all other substantial economies.

These averages hide some important details. The living standards of ordinary Australians increased more than those of the rich through most of the twentieth century. The inequality of incomes widened after 1980, although government policies offset this up to the end of the century. In the early twenty-first century, Australia has become less equal even when changes in government policy are taken into account, mirroring the rest of the developed world – but less markedly so than in the United States and the United Kingdom.

But still, ordinary Australians were earning more in 2011 than they ever had. We now face a great challenge to these conditions. We will not be able to hold on to all of the gains of the past two decades in the immediate future. However, a combination of good leadership, sound analysis and the successful assertion of the public interest in policy will allow us to preserve much and eventually return to growth after the current challenges are met. The question is: will we face up to them and make the decisions that need to be made in the public interest?

RESOURCES BOOMS RAISE INCOMES BUT LEAVE PROBLEMS

Throughout Australia's history, strong growth in the industrial economies, and the high resource prices flowing from this, has brought prosperity and often economic boomtime. Subsequent downturns in the industrial economies were then transmitted with magnified force into Australia, leading to slumps that were usually followed by long periods of stagnation and high unemployment.

The mostly strong global growth from the 1850s to the collapse of 1891 kept wool and other commodity prices high, and the London financial markets loved lending to Australian governments and banks. By the 1880s, a resources boom ran alongside a housing boom. Australian asset prices rose to levels that could be sustained only while commodity prices remained high and the flow of London credit strong.

The boom ended when the collapse of resources prices was accompanied by the drying up of international credit. 'The price of wool was falling,' begins the 'Ballad of 1891', describing how pressures to cut wages in depression precipitated the great shearers' strike that led to the formation of the Australian Labor Party. The sharpest decline in activity and employment in Australia before or since followed.

After the trauma of the early 1890s, the democratic Australian colonies yearned to be free of the vagaries of the international economy. These pressures were crucial to the 'Australian Settlement' in the years around Federation, where protection against imports, wage arbitration and widespread government regulation of business decisions and ownership became distinctive features of our economy. Protection increased with each passing decade until well into the second half of the twentieth century. The young Australian economics profession in the 1920s obliged the country's political preferences by developing a unique and analytically unsatisfactory 'Australian case for protection'.

The same democratic institutions that protected Australia from an early Latin American-style 'locking up of the land' also prevented the large-scale immigration of low-cost labour from Asia. The first acts of the new Federal Parliament in 1901 excluded non-white migrants comprehensively. Subsequent interpretation of the White Australia Policy tightly restricted immigration from southern Europe before World War II.

Australia was tied to the fortunes of the United Kingdom by sentiment, institutions and (from the early years of the Great Depression) preferential trade agreements. We therefore shared the United Kingdom's economic underperformance through the three decades from the outbreak of World War I in 1914 to peace after 1945.

Sluggish growth in Australia's main market, the burdens of high protection, poorly conceived regulation and public investment, and a legacy of public debt from World War I all contributed to stagnation. From 1927, clear-minded observers could see troubles ahead. Australia's problems were then overlaid by the Great Depression from 1929. As in 1891, the collapse of resource prices coincided with the freezing of access to international credit to produce an economic crisis.

Unlike in 1891, deliberate if tentative policies were adopted in response: a large currency devaluation against the British pound (which had itself depreciated against gold and the US dollar); limited expansion of public works as unemployment relief; wage and interest rate cuts; and measures to ease the burden on the unemployed. These policies were conceived within an explicit if incomplete framework of shared sacrifice. They were developed, with the assistance of most leading economists, by the Scullin Labor government in its dying days in 1931 and implemented by the Lyons conservative government. The new policies helped bring about a recovery more rapid than in Britain and much more so than in the United States.

The Great Depression left a legacy of even more pervasive regulation and diminished prospects for economic growth. The regulation of external trade and payments was extended during World War II, and its aftermath saw restrictions continue in response to foreign exchange shortages in the British-led Sterling Currency Area, of which Australia was part.

A spike in demand for wool in 1950 and 1951, with tension and then war on the Korean Peninsula, lifted Australia's terms of trade to unprecedented heights. The temporary surge in export prices generated a burst of high inflation. These were Salad Days of economic policy. The economists' Keynesian insights from the 1930s were moulded into policy by advisers brought together under Curtin and Chifley and retained by Menzies after 1949. The community grumbled but was tolerant of restrictions on short-term private consumption for long-term national gain. After a short and shallow recession, inflation quickly fell to low levels. The second of Australia's long booms followed, lasting till the early 1970s (only broken by a brief recession in 1960–61). Until the late 1960s, the country saw high productivity growth by previous standards – although it was well below contemporary performance in other developed countries. There were only modest expectations of rising incomes, combined with consistently low unemployment alongside high immigration and population growth.

A JAPAN RESOURCES BOOM FOLLOWED BY INSTABILITY

The early restoration of healthy trade and diplomatic relations with Japan after the war was an achievement with economic as well as strategic dimensions. Japan's post-war industrialisation brought the centre of gravity of the global economy closer to Australia. Reduced transport costs created new opportunities for the export of bulk commodities: iron ore, coal, and raw and lightly processed aluminium and nickel ores. Through the 1960s, small towns grew rapidly and new towns appeared in remote regions of northern and western Australia.

Australia's terms of trade rose in the early 1970s to the highest levels since the Korean War boom as Japan's industrial growth approached its apogee, and energy prices were lifted by restrictions of oil supply in the Middle East. Our terms of trade increased by 46 per cent in three years from December 1971 (a low point). Australia spent most of the higher income as the money was received. Between September 1970 and September 1974, a burst of inflation and belated currency appreciation lifted the real exchange rate by what was then an unprecedented 17 per cent. The Australian econometrician Adrian Pagan, cited by Ian McLean in an important recent economic history of Australia, described this rise in the real exchange rate as 'disastrous' and as bringing the postwar boom to an end.

The higher oil prices were the immediate trigger for a global slump. The developed countries in the northern hemisphere entered recession, and Japan shifted gears from rapid to moderate growth in 1974. Commodity prices declined swiftly, leaving Australia hopelessly uncompetitive with its high real exchange rate. The nominal exchange rate fell from late 1974, but real incomes didn't, which entrenched high inflation despite recession. Australia entered nine years of low growth, high inflation and unemployment.

These years of economic instability incorporated a brief resources boom from 1979 to 1981. The restriction of Middle Eastern oil supplies from 1979 in the Iran–Iraq War encouraged export-oriented investment in thermal coal for the first time. Japan sent its energy-intensive and highly polluting industries offshore, which underpinned investment in aluminium smelting in Australia.

The collapse of this boom in 1982 again left Australia with a cost structure that was out of line with global economic reality. Unemployment rose to a new post-war peak in early 1983, while inflation remained high.

TWO PRECONDITIONS FOR REFORM

The economic disappointments between 1974 and 1983 were followed by a remarkable Reform Era. This began with the election of the Hawke Labor government in March 1983. It reached its apogee in 1989–91. It was weakened by a deep recession in 1990–91 and the long period of high unemployment that followed. It ended following the political contest over the Goods and Services Tax (GST) in 2000.

What made the Reform Era possible? One precondition was the abolition of the White Australia Policy. Discriminatory immigration had stood in the way of productive relations with Australia's neighbours in Asia. A second precondition was growing understanding in the populace of the need for economic reform if Australians were to continue to enjoy the living standards of modern developed countries.

The first breach in the White Australia Policy was made by the Holt Coalition government in 1966. The Whitlam Labor government brought racial discrimination in immigration formally to an end in 1973, but the practical effects of this were diminished by big cuts in the number of migrants. The Fraser Coalition government ushered in large-scale non-European immigration for the first time since Federation with a politically courageous decision to accept substantial numbers of refugees from Indochina. The White Australia Policy was laid to rest in practice as well as in principle in the mid-1980s, when the Hawke government applied the new non-discriminatory policies to a large-scale immigration programme.

Each of these steps was made possible through public education and advocacy by informed members of the community – private people across the partisan political divide coming together to promote a change in policy that was judged to be in the public interest. An informed independent centre of the polity created a climate of opinion in which it was possible for leaders to make changes. However, four prime ministers over two decades had to absorb bitter criticism from parts of the community, to accept political costs and to take political risks.

The centrepiece of economic reform, and the area subject to strongest opposition from business and trade union interests, was the winding back of protection. Awareness of the costs of protection and the benefits of reform began with independent analysis, at first by a small number of people in the universities. The analysis was extended and publicised from the late 1960s by the Tariff Board (the predecessor of today's Productivity Commission).

From its formation in the 1920s, the Tariff Board had mostly been comfortable working within the established consensus on protection. It changed in the late 1960s, under the leadership of individuals who asserted their independence from government and business pressures and were prepared to take bold professional stands in the public interest.

The work of academic economists and the Tariff Board was introduced to the wider Australian community by a small number of journalists, who put effort into understanding and explaining complex arguments, and who were allowed to do so by their editors, boards of directors and proprietors.

By the mid-1970s there was an understanding of the costs of protection to the Australian standard of living within a substantial group of independent and public interest-oriented citizens – 'elite opinion', as it came to be characterised by some political leaders and commentators in the early twenty-first century. There was widespread although by no means universal understanding that Australian economic performance had been relatively poor.

There was widespread but by no means universal understanding of the value of far-reaching changes. There was widespread but by no means universal understanding that the necessary changes included reducing barriers to the international exchange of finance, goods and services.

Independent reports commissioned by governments widened public understanding of the need for and benefits of reform. The Fraser government's Campbell Committee Report helped to build understanding of the value of financial reform. Although the Fraser government itself did not implement many of the report's recommendations, together with the Hawke government's own Martin Report it was an important part of the background to the swift and comprehensive reforms in the mid-1980s. My own *Australia and the Northeast Asian Ascendancy*, presented to Prime Minister Bob Hawke in October 1989, caught the public imagination by linking opportunities in Asia to reform at home. The Hilmer Report in 1993 helped build support for the widening of the scope of competition policy into the states following major advances in the commonwealth from 1987.

Cutting back protection allowed the Australian government to participate actively in multilateral trade negotiations for the first time. In turn, this supported the inclusion of agriculture among measures to reduce global protection. Australia's sponsorship of Asia-Pacific Economic Cooperation from 1989 and its promotion of the idea of 'open regionalism' (regional trade liberalisation without discrimination against outsiders) was an important influence on many Western Pacific countries up to the Asian Financial Crisis of 1997–98.

When it came to winding back protection, there never was anything like majority support. Protection remained popular even when its removal was playing a major role in increasing Australian living standards during the 1990s and 2000s. Vested interests were well organised to spend heavily to block reform through lobbying, donations to political parties and public presentation of arguments against reform.

Nevertheless, through the Reform Era, the influence of both popular opinion and vested interests on the policy process was constrained by the presence of a substantial, well-informed independent centre of the polity. This independent centre ensured that leaders seeking political advantage by pandering to populist or vested interests would suffer harm to their reputations. It also ensured that a leader wishing to make major change in the public interest would have support.

REFORM AND THE RECESSION WE DIDN'T HAVE TO HAVE

The willingness of Australians to accept change increased during the economic instability of 1974 to 1983. Hawke took office just as unemployment rose to its highest level since the Great Depression, reaching 10.3 per cent in

March 1983 and remaining there until September. Jobs were the first priority of the new government; structural change to raise long-term growth would proceed slowly until people were confident that employment was growing. But structural change to promote long-term growth was part of the government's story about itself from April 1983: some steps were taken along that track from the May Statement of 1983, and few steps were taken that were inconsistent with the long-term direction.

Economic performance through the reform period breaks into three contrasting parts. The first seven years saw strong growth driven by the expansion of employment: from June 1983 until June 1990, economic output increased by 37 per cent and employment (total hours worked) by 29 per cent. By contrast, in the preceding nine years, output had increased by 21 per cent, and in the five years to June 1983 (collection of these data began only in 1978), employment had increased by a mere 2 per cent.

Prosperity was threatened in the mid-1980s by a large fall in the terms of trade, which took the exchange rate down with it. This was the first episode of a weak dollar after the floating of the exchange rate. It created alarm at the time, and was used by the government to galvanise action on reform. The low exchange rate of these years helped the winding back of protection.

Late in the 1980s, domestic spending began to grow at historically high rates, fuelled by a lift in the terms of trade and rapid credit expansion. Fiscal policy was firm from 1984 and tight in the late '80s, with budget surpluses around 1.5 per cent of GDP – but not tight enough to offset the boom in private spending. Interest rates were raised again and again. The real exchange rate rose by one-third from a trough in September 1986 to a peak in September 1990. The vigorous expansion of manufactures and services exports from the beginning of the Reform Era now stopped.

Interest rate increases continued after political crises in the Soviet Union and China and then recession in the northern developed countries caused export prices to fall. In a familiar Australian pattern, the retreat of temporarily high terms of trade and the puncturing of a boom in debt-funded spending combined to cause recession. Monetary policy was tightened too late to stop the emergence of boom conditions, and then excessively and for too long so that it precipitated a deep recession.

This was the second part of the economic story of the reform era: the deep recession of 1990–91. Output fell by 1.6 per cent from peak to trough. Employment (monthly hours worked per adult) started falling earlier than output, fell more and kept falling for longer. Unemployment, which had fallen below 6 per cent in 1989, rose quickly to a new post-Great Depression peak of 11.2 per cent in December 1992.

There were two silver linings. The recession ended the high inflation that had persisted for two decades. But the costs were substantial: the loss of value in the recession itself; persistent long-term unemployment through much of the 1990s; the corrosion of skills; and the loss of confidence in market-oriented reform. We did not have to have the deep recession. Low inflation could have been purchased at a much lower cost.

The second silver lining was that leaders relinquished political control of monetary policy. Both the large increases in interest rates of the 1980s and the timing and extent of their easing were closely associated with Treasurer Paul Keating and the Hawke government. It is unlikely that the policy would have been different at this time if administered by an independent Reserve Bank: perceptions did not vary much across the senior echelons of the official family. However, after the recession no one in government wanted to argue for continued control of monetary policy. The Reserve Bank quietly assumed, then asserted, its independence. This was formalised by the incoming Howard Coalition government in 1996.

In the third part of the economic story of the Reform Era, Australia enjoyed the first half of its long boom. It entered the longest period of expansion unbroken by recession in its history – or in the modern history of any developed economy. The last decade of the Reform Era was characterised by low inflation. From the recession of 1990–91 through to 2000, Australian total productivity growth was the highest in the developed world, after being close to the lowest through most of the twentieth century.

REFORM FOR OPENNESS AND EQUITY

The removal of old barriers to trade began early and made Australians aware that they were living in an economy in which the relevant benchmarks were the best international practice.

Reductions in protection were gradual, with important decisions being taken each year from 1983 to 1991. First came the removal of quantitative restrictions on steel and a number of other major products. Large across-the-board cuts in tariffs were announced in 1988 and 1991. The March 1991 Statement, delivered in deep recession, covered the single largest step in the dismantling of protection: phased reductions extending to 1996 for most goods and to 2000 for the most highly protected.

Other major distortions were removed in 1983 and 1984: the system for allocating crude oil that had separated the domestic and international energy markets; and the requirement for government approval of the terms of all export sales of major resource commodities. Comprehensive regulation of prices and quantities for rural producers – notably the dairy industry – was removed in successive steps through the 1980s. From sharing with New Zealand the distinction of having the highest protection against imported goods (agricultural and industrial products together) of all developed countries in the early 1980s, by the mid-1990s Australia with New Zealand had the lowest.

The reforms led to even greater change in our international trade in services. Changes in education policy supported by adjustments to immigration in the mid-1980s saw the emergence of education as a major export industry. The removal of exchange controls led to direct overseas investment by Australian-based firms, which facilitated the rapid growth of a range of service exports. Civil aviation reforms were important to the rapid growth of tourism, with the ratio of inbound to outbound visits doubling over the period.

Financial reforms were commenced in 1983 and mostly completed by 1985: the removal of all foreign exchange controls and the floating of the dollar in December 1983; the removal of controls on interest rates; and the issue of licences for new foreign-owned banks for the first time since early in the twentieth century and on a scale without precedent.

Despite the high real exchange rate of the late 1980s, export volumes grew at a compound rate of over 7 per cent per annum throughout the Reform Era. Services and manufactures exports grew most rapidly. By the end of this time, Australia had a diverse range of exports, with similar contributions from services, resources, manufactures and rural products.

From 1983 until the end of the century, there was far-reaching public finance reform: the targeting of social security on people with lower incomes and without large assets; restraint in spending and removal of tax concessions as part of a strategy to balance the commonwealth budget over the economic cycle; the first commitment by an Australian government to limits on revenue, expenditure and the deficit as a share of the economy in Hawke's 'Trilogy' of 1984; cuts in income tax alongside the broadening of the tax base to cover previously exempt (capital gains, 'fringe benefits') and largely exempt (superannuation) income; resource rent taxes for projects within commonwealth jurisdictions; and the replacement of the wholesale sales tax, and some state-based taxes and a small part of the income tax, by a broadly based value-added tax introduced by the Howard government in 2000.

Budget data was presented in new ways that allowed informed discussion of government finances. Forward estimates of revenue and expenditure were published from the mid-1980s. Early in the life of the Howard government a 'Charter of Budget Honesty' was introduced that required half-yearly release of budget estimates, with another such update to be made available by the secretaries for Finance and Treasury within ten days of an election being called.

The reform agenda covered the corporatisation of many public enterprises (which were required to operate independently in a competitive environment) and eventually the sale of almost all commonwealth businesses. Some states followed suit with the privatisation of utilities. Privatisation was preceded by careful work on regulatory policy in transport and communications. This was open to scrutiny as a basis for public discussion, and provided the foundations for a subsequent extension of competition policy.

The reform agenda included a large increase in investment in education, training, research and development. The proportions of Australians completing high school and tertiary education increased from below to above the average for developed countries.

There were also changes in taxation and provision of public services to support more equitable access. Most important were Medicare and support for low-income families with children. (The latter was of immense social significance, although derided for falling short of Prime Minister Hawke's election statement that after its introduction no Australian child would live in poverty.) The cost of these was partly covered by income and asset testing of social security payments.

Labour-market reform in the early 1990s increased flexibility in setting wages and employment conditions. This was taken forward moderately by the Howard government in 1996, long before its step too far after the 2004 election.

There was one major move away from economically rational policies in 1999, which in some ways was an augury of the end of the Reform Era: a cut in the capital-gains tax rate, which reopened old opportunities for tax avoidance.

Most of the productivity-raising reforms were fiercely opposed by interests that stood to lose from them, by influential parts of the press and by majority popular opinion. Every one of the changes in isolation was politically difficult and offered an opportunity for rival parties to win short-term gains through opposition.

THE HELPFUL MYTH OF BIPARTISAN SUPPORT

A mostly helpful myth has developed that the Reform Era was characterised by bipartisan support for change. The reality is more varied and complex. The financial liberalisation can be fairly characterised as having had bipartisan support, most importantly from the shadow treasurer and later leader of the Opposition, John Howard. Cutting back protection had the active support of a minority of Liberal federal parliamentarians through the 1980s, but not comprehensive support until the elevation of John Hewson to the leadership after the 1990 election. Hewson accepted the recommendation in *Australia and the Northeast Asian Ascendancy* that Australia should remove all remaining protection by 2000. This provided political support for Prime Minister Hawke's March 1991 Statement.

By contrast, the Opposition made rejection of the government's measures to expand the tax base, and to target pensions more tightly, central planks of its 1984 election platform.

The reality was less complex when the Howard government took office in 1996. The Labor Opposition opposed moderate further steps towards a more flexible labour market in 1996. It gave support to cutting the capital-gains tax rate in half. It then opposed fiercely the government's broader package of taxation reform incorporating a GST. Australia entered a period of policy populism in which bipartisan support was common for measures that favoured private and sectional interests, but rare for productivity-raising reform.

REFORM REQUIRES A NEW POLITICAL CULTURE

The quality of political leadership on both sides of the Parliament was crucial to the success of the Reform Era. From the beginning, the Hawke government sought to reorient Australian political culture. Hawke saw the disorganisation of the Whitlam Cabinet and its tendency to surprise the public with new policy announcements, and the social tension and conflict under Fraser, as causes of policy failure. He was determined to govern with order and without surprises, and with the support of as wide a spectrum of the community as possible. 'Cooperation' and 'consensus', 'shared information' and 'shared understanding' were guiding concepts.

The Hawke government came to office with an 'Accord' with the trade union movement. The parties to the Accord were committed to close cooperation to achieve high employment and strong growth. It was understood that success would require incomes restraint in the early years, which was to be secured within a framework of fair distribution.

A National Economic Summit Conference within the first two months of the new government brought together business, trade union and social welfare leaders, and provided them with the bureaucracy's assessments of the economic outlook and policy choices as a basis for wider discussion.

Successive speeches of the prime minister in his first year of office emphasised the importance of trade and financial liberalisation, and productivity-raising investment in education, research and development, while tying them to opportunities for a more internationally oriented economy that would take advantage of the growth of East Asia in general and China in particular.

The breadth and depth of the agenda required the decentralisation of ministerial leadership. Here the prime minister's leadership style suited the demands of the reform programme. In the presence of the relevant advisers in his office and often from his department, Hawke would discuss policy issues with ministers and lay out objectives for the portfolio in major speeches. The ministers would then be given considerable responsibility for carrying out the reforms, consulting regularly with the prime minister and his office, and taking submissions to Cabinet when proposals had been defined.

The exceptional quality of ministers in the Hawke Cabinet made the depth and breadth of the reform programme and the decentralisation of responsibility possible. Hawke used his own personal staff and department effectively. The

Department of the Prime Minister and Cabinet comprised public servants of high quality, many of whom had backgrounds in policy departments. Its roles were to coordinate the prime minister's relations with other departments on policy matters, to ensure that he had access to the advice that other departments were providing to their ministers, and to provide separate advice on important issues. Hawke used a small personal policy staff productively – in the early years, a chief of staff with deep experience in the Department of Foreign Affairs and the Treasury, and with confident access across the public service; one economic adviser on the main policy issues (the author until September 1985); one foreign affairs adviser; two political advisers to maintain contact with the caucus and party; and an effective media office. Other specialist policy officers were added later, including an adviser on the environment.

There was also administrative reorganisation to support analysis and public education for reform. An Economic Policy Advisory Council (EPAC) continued the work of the Summit. An EPAC secretariat undertook research on reform issues, drawing on the resources of the public service and making papers available to the public. After the 1984 election, a Cabinet Committee on Long-Term Economic Growth was established, with a brief to develop a programme of far-reaching reform.

Through the mid-1980s a political culture emerged in which it was possible to undertake massive change in policy with large implications for economic structure that inevitably imposed costs on some groups. Vested interests still sought sectoral advantage, but accepted there was no point in putting forward a policy that could not be supported by rigorous analysis on public interest grounds. The Business Council and the Australian Council of Trade Unions declined to support individual members' positions that could not be defended rigorously on such grounds. Economic arguments for policy reform in the national interest became familiar to the public. The treasurer, Paul Keating, quipped that the galahs in every pet shop were squawking about micro-economic reform.

Sectoral business organisations, beginning with the National Farmers' Federation, pursued their own objectives by stressing the contribution that the changes they were seeking made to the public interest. They reduced demands that could not be defended credibly in this framework. Different political groups watched over the intellectual quality of contributions by others to the public discussion; to make a case, an interest group required not only a supporting argument from an economist, but also a credible and logical argument that could stand up to professional scrutiny.

When the government proposed new steps in reform, these were already familiar to many in the community, so that there was a base for wider public education, and opposition was constrained by knowledge. It seemed that a new political culture had made the search for more productive ways of doing things an integral part of Australian life.

CHAPTER 3
THE GREAT AUSTRALIAN COMPLACENCY

'There is a good chance that Australians are about to receive the biggest economic shock of the last several decades,' I said to the Australia Unlimited Conference in May 1999. 'The evidence is gathering, and may soon be too strong to be denied, that Australians in 1999 are living through the third period in the century since Federation of sustained economic prosperity.' Prime Minister Howard liked the remarks and referred to them many times inside and outside Parliament over the next few months.

Three years later, my opening address to the first Economic and Social Outlook Conference at the University of Melbourne told a story of Australia's victory late in the twentieth century over the inward-looking policies that had held us back from Federation until the 1980s. 'The greatly improved economic performance of Australia through the period of internationally oriented reform,' I said, 'provides a basis for an optimistic view of Australia's 21st-century prospects.'

I wasn't unqualifiedly optimistic: 'Australia is likely to experience all three of continued economic reform, equitable distribution and strong economic growth, or none of them.'

The prosperity kept growing. It is still present in the latest data available as this book goes to print in October 2013. But the sources of growth changed suddenly from the turn of the century. We gave up reform and found that we had given up productivity growth as well. Executive pay, profits and wages grew at an accelerated rate and employment kept expanding because fortuitous and temporary events sheltered us from what would otherwise have been the consequences of the end of productivity growth.

This turned out to be an unfavourable environment for reform-oriented political culture. The easy success in the economy went along with a decline in public support for rational economic policy. Interest groups became more overt and effective in applying pressure to the policymaking process. These developments made productivity-raising and stability-enhancing reform in the public interest a historical relic. Everything that interest groups demanded in the way of new policy and everything that governments did on the economy was still described as 'reform', but few of the proposed changes had much prospect of getting us to do things more efficiently.

By 2004, I was drawing attention not to the surprise of continued strong growth, but to the vulnerability of the growth that Australians were now taking for granted. 'So there is a considerable chance,' I said in my Melville Lecture in December, 'that the current vulnerability to large external or domestic shocks will continue … We would be wise to reduce vulnerability in the period ahead … It would help if fiscal policy were now tightened considerably.'

From 2004, I was describing the period following the Reform Era as the Great Australian Complacency. In my presentation to the Economic and Social Outlook Conference in March 2005, I noted that both the reform and the rapid productivity growth of the 1990s had stopped.

Despite the stagnation of productivity, economic growth had continued for several years after the turn of the century because our banks were borrowing at unprecedented rates in international markets to lend for housing and consumption. We would have to return to the hard work of reform or face the even harder reality of falling living standards when international markets called a halt to our growing debt, and commodity prices reverted to something closer to the levels of the late twentieth century.

'As a community we accepted the excellent economic performance as evidence that we had changed enough,' I said in that same presentation in early 2005.

> Our community has never been comfortable with the application of professional economic analysis to policy choice – so-called 'economic rationalism' – but for a while, from 1983 to the turn of the century, had been persuaded of its necessity. Now Australians have reverted to their traditional preference for having popular politics in command of resource allocation and economic policy-making. The links were forgotten between earlier economic reform and the contemporary prosperity.
>
> Economic analysis was banished to the periphery of many areas of policy-making. Endorsement by business interests and economists hired to argue a case for politically preferred policies again became more important than transparent analysis … The return to populism in economic policy-making has had bipartisan support at federal level …

The Great Complacency began to be challenged only from 2013, after more than a year of declining employment relative to population, through public discussion of the end of the China boom. Over the next couple of years, we will learn what has replaced it.

The story of the Great Australian Complacency is as important as the story of the Reform Era. Like the Reform Era, the Great Australian Complacency has its origins in the relationship between the state of the economy and ideas about how the economy works; in political leadership and the dynamics of electoral competition; in the wider political culture's resistance to or support for sectional pressures for policy change; and in the preparedness of people in the independent centre of the polity to make personal efforts in the public interest, along with the quality and effectiveness of those efforts.

THE GST AND THE END OF THE REFORM ERA

The Australian economy grew more slowly during the Asian Financial Crisis of 1997–98. It would have entered recession but for the falling dollar and the decision of the Reserve Bank not to raise interest rates despite the inflation coming from a falling dollar.

The introduction of the GST was part of a larger set of taxation changes in 2000 that increased consumer and business uncertainty, even though the 'compensation' for the tax exceeded what it brought in by a full percentage point of GDP (the equivalent of $15 billion today). Australian GDP fell in one quarter and remained subdued for a year.

For want of a better one, this book applies the standard definition of a recession: two successive quarters of declining output. This definition sets a low bar for avoiding recession in Australia because of our growing population. Real output per person can fall for several quarters without attracting the label of recession.

The Howard government was under electoral pressure at the time the GST was introduced in mid-2000.

The Coalition had won government in 1998 with a minority of the two-party preferred vote, and was well behind in the opinion polls leading up to the 2001 general election. It loosened fiscal policy beyond the massive overcompensation of the tax package itself, including through incentives for home ownership and ending indexation of the petrol excise. The new incentives for home ownership contributed to a boom in house prices, which emerged at the same time as similar developments in other English-speaking countries and Spain. The effects of the cut in petrol excise gradually accumulated over time until by 2013 it exceeded $5 billion dollars per annum. The 2001 election also gave rise to tax cuts and social security increases.

WE SHOULD HAVE SAVED MORE

After the year of subdued growth, economic output bounced back to over 3 per cent and mostly over 4 per cent for the next several years. The higher growth was concentrated in housing and consumption. Household savings fell to near zero, despite large increases in income. The boom in domestic spending was accompanied by a large increase in the terms of trade from 2003, as China's demand for resources gathered steam. As the extra revenue arrived, governments spent most of it in the form of tax cuts and increased transfer payments and other expenditure. This added to the debt-funded boom.

The government maintained a surplus of about 1.5 per cent of GDP for several years. This was about the rate during the boom years of the late 1980s, which had turned out to be insufficient for stabilisation – and the early 2000s was a much bigger boom. The current account deficit rose to its highest ever share of GDP at around 6 per cent, despite export prices rising to historically high levels. This was funded to a considerable extent by off-shore wholesale borrowing by the banks. High domestic spending and firm monetary policy caused the real exchange rate to rise markedly, which brought to an end the vigorous growth in services and manufactures exports that had been a feature of the Australian economy since the beginning of the Reform Era.

While Australian incomes and employment were growing strongly, import prices were falling due to the rising dollar and cheaper consumer goods from China. Prices for domestic products increased by about 4 per cent per annum from early in the new century to 2013, making a massive cumulative contribution to the decline in international competitiveness.

Australia had entered a domestic expenditure boom and rising real exchange rate, fuelled by foreign debt and high terms of trade. This set of economic changes had much in common with those in the early 1890s, late 1920s, early 1970s and late 1980s that had preceded collapse, followed by long periods of high unemployment and sluggish growth.

The changes of the Reform Era helped to keep growth going and inflation low. The floating dollar moved down decisively and sheltered industries through the Asian Financial Crisis. It floated up to insulate inflation rates from the domestic expenditure boom. A more flexible labour market reduced unemployment associated with the Asian Financial Crisis and the slump around the introduction of the GST.

But for those who remembered Australian vulnerability to the collapse of credit at times of international financial stress, the high current account deficits, increasing external debt and heavy reliance on wholesale credit markets were a source of concern. The extraordinarily high real exchange rate also caused anxiety for those who recalled the political difficulty, extended timetables, and high unemployment and loss of economic output involved in lowering an unrealistically high cost structure.

Different views emerged within the economics profession about what was needed to maintain stability. The majority, official and influential view at this time was that the changes of the Reform Era – the floating currency and the more flexible labour market together with the avoidance of deficits on government account – meant that the emerging circumstances of the early twenty-first century were of no concern.

According to the dominant view, the floating exchange rate had appreciated when the terms of trade and domestic expenditure were strong. It would float down when the economy required a lower rate. The independent Reserve Bank would tighten monetary policy to combat inflation, and loosen it if expenditure fell below levels that were necessary to maintain full employment.

We were running budget surpluses; any current account deficit was the result of private expenditure exceeding private income. It was therefore the result of decisions by consenting adults. Private businesses would not borrow if the debts that they were incurring could not be repaid out of earnings. And if some private borrowers from international markets ran into difficulties, that would be a problem for them and those who lent to them, not for the general community or the government.

The alternative view was weakly represented, if at all, within the official family. Economists of this persuasion, including myself, argued that much more of the government revenue from the high terms of trade should be saved and stored. This would do three things. It would reduce the current account deficit. The accumulated savings would give us a large buffer against credit markets suddenly closing and making it impossible to service the large external liabilities that Australia was accumulating. And it would reduce the rise in the real exchange rate by holding down domestic spending, and so obviate the need for painful and risky adjustment at a later date.

For economists putting forward this alternative view, it was little comfort that the accumulating private debt was held in the private sector. Australia's own history of financial crises and the recent experience of the Asian Financial Crisis showed that problems in financing large accumulations of private international credit could seriously damage national economic performance. Problems of private debt were quickly socialised in hard times.

The two views were laid out at length and debated in a meeting of a Senate Committee set up for this purpose in 2005. In the event, the Australian government was comfortable with leaving things where they were. Meanwhile reform had come to an end and productivity was declining. The Great Australian Complacency had permeated the whole of economic policy.

THE GREAT CRASH IN AUSTRALIA

The first signs of problems in the financial systems of the United States and the United Kingdom emerged in 2007. However, China's investment-led growth continued apace and took Australia's terms of trade to new heights through 2007 and the first seven months of 2008. The largest of all the tax cuts was offered by the Howard government and largely matched by the Opposition in the lead-up to the October 2007 election. Strong growth in output continued. The labour market was as fully employed as it had ever been in July 2008: monthly hours of work per person over fifteen years, 90.7 hours, reached the highest level recorded since the Bureau of Statistics began publishing the series in 1978. Competitive pressures and the demonstration effect of easy fortunes made from financial innovation in the northern hemisphere were influencing the behaviour of Australian financial institutions; the governor of the Reserve Bank, Glenn Stevens, remarked in 2013 that Australia was fortunate the Great Crash of 2008 occurred before bad practices were more deeply entrenched here.

But we were less damagingly exposed to financial risk for positive as well as negative reasons: the Australian financial system had never had the extreme deregulation of the United States and the authorities had warned of the dangers of excess from the middle of the decade.

Suddenly, in September 2008, even highly rated Australian private banks were unable to borrow from the international wholesale market. On a Sunday afternoon in October, the Rudd Labor government responded to the distress of the banks by guaranteeing all their wholesale debts, eventually taking on a contingent liability of $178 billion for a fee that was minuscule in comparison with the value contributed by the government's intervention.

This enormous and timely intervention saved our banks from financial failure. Recession was avoided by massive fiscal and monetary expansion in Australia, as well as our trading partners, most importantly China. The competitiveness of exports was maintained by quick and large depreciation of the Australian dollar.

THE BOOM RESUMES

By the end of 2009 the Chinese economy was growing strongly again and Australia's terms of trade were back to their earlier heights and rising. Growth in output resumed after a single quarter of decline. In contrast with almost all other developed countries, unemployment remained low.

Again, the flexible exchange rate and the more flexible labour market supported fiscal and monetary policy in maintaining growth through the most challenging circumstances. Australia narrowly missed great stress, but the absence of recession and the early return of high prosperity confirmed for us that ours was the best of all possible worlds.

Fiscal policy was tight by historical standards after the Rudd government's stimulus in response to the Great Crash. Indeed, in 2012–13, leading into an election, nominal (that is, in dollars and not only in real purchasing power) commonwealth expenditure actually fell for the first time in the forty years in which Treasury data are available in comparable forms. This amounted to a fall of over 3 per cent in real terms, or 5 per cent per capita, following a smaller fall in real terms in 2011–12. In contrast with longstanding practice before the Great Crash, the government went to an election without offering income tax cuts, and the Opposition matched the restraint.

The budget deficit for 2012–13 came down a long way from 2.9 per cent of GDP in 2011–12, but the remaining 1.3 per cent of GDP was a long way short of the surplus that had appeared in the original budget estimates. Extraordinary expenditure restraint could not keep up with the decline in corporate income tax and the shortfall in resource rent tax after the resources boom turned from positive to negative in 2011.

While budgets were firm after 2009, a tighter budget and lower interest rates from early 2010 would have taken some of the edge off the exchange rate appreciation. But there can be no credible argument that the budget was too loose from mid-2011. In retrospect, interest rates were kept too high under the circumstances of contraction from the resources sector and the commonwealth budget.

After the Great Crash, household savings returned to the higher levels of the Reform Era, at around 10 per cent of income. This helped to hold external debt at merely high levels as resources investment attained great momentum in 2010. As it became clear that Australia had escaped the severe economic problems of most of the developed world, boom-time seemed to have become permanent. It was unnecessary to heed the caution of a few economists about the problem of competitiveness.

CHALLENGES TO THE LEGITIMACY OF REFORM

The strong growth in jobs in the early years of the Reform Era had conferred legitimacy on reform. More people accepted at face value statements about the effects of further reform by Prime Minister Bob Hawke and Treasurer Paul Keating.

This source of legitimacy disappeared with the recession in 1990–91. While recession should be expected when short-term interest rates approach 20 per cent and the terms of trade are falling, its arrival surprised the government and was hardly anticipated in the media or by big business. Forewarned is forearmed, and Australians walked into the worst downturn since the Great Depression without protection. Surprise and the absence of an official explanation made the recession especially damaging to the government's reputation for good economic management.

Many people who had been uneasy about reform but silent or ineffective while the new policies seemed to be delivering good outcomes were quick to blame reform for recession. 'Economic rationalism' became a widely used term of abuse. The Labor government, in its last few years, stopped contesting the critique. Government spokespeople would explain to outsiders that this was not an 'economic rationalist' government. The apparent retreat from the application of economic analysis to policy increased the vulnerability of good policy to pressure from populist as well as vested interests.

There is a strand of modern economics that is extreme in its assertion that markets should not be subject to regulation and, as a corollary, that there is no place for concern for equity in policy. This strand, accurately described as libertarian, has a much smaller place in the professional study of economics than in the popular discourse, but nevertheless has proponents in the discipline.

Libertarian views played a role in the extreme financial deregulation of the United States and United Kingdom that contributed to the global financial crisis in 2008. But libertarianism has never had a significant place in Australian economic analysis, and was not influential in policymaking during the Reform Era. (Senior figures at the Institute of Public Affairs have recently been describing themselves as libertarian, and may be a vehicle through which extreme views about the role of government become influential for the first time.)

Australian financial reform was characterised by a strong focus on prudential regulation of a kind that was rejected in the United States and the United Kingdom. This contributed to the Australian financial system's relatively strong position through the global financial crisis.

The reaction against the application of economic analysis to policy was assisted by two developments within the economics profession itself. From its earliest days, Australian economists had seen the discipline as a social science, the value of which was measured by its capacity to illuminate developments in the world and be relevant to policy. Over recent decades there has been a large movement away from this tradition. Indeed, relevance to Australian reality and policy has become a drawback for professional advancement. A focus on being published in high-impact 'international' journals – in practice mostly US publications – led to a low professional value being placed on contributions to understanding Australian reality. This discouraged younger academic economists in Australia from work on local policy.

The second development has been the commercialisation of contributions by professional economists. The culture of Australian economics was once set by academic traditions of independence from vested interests. By the early twenty-first century, most contributions to the policy discussion were made by economists employed directly by, or as consultants to, business.

Some business economists – for example, most of those employed by banks – were usually not required to promote specific policy proposals. However, their incentive structures favoured focus on short-term matters: What will the Reserve Bank do to interest rates at its next meeting? What will the next monthly unemployment figures reveal? What will be the value of the Australian dollar at the end of the year? Other economists had specific policy briefs from their employers. Their work was riddled with undeclared conflicts of interest.

Sound, disinterested analysis of long-term policy issues was crowded out by daily commentary and the noisy firing of the hired guns of business and political interests. Through the Great Complacency, gruesome examples abounded of economists capable of better things undertaking work of low professional quality on a commercial basis to assist businesses and lobbies that had employed them for this purpose. I mention two cases, not because they were more problematic than others, but because they illustrate two dimensions of the problem.

A paper prepared for the Department of Foreign Affairs and Trade by well-known economic consultants demonstrated that in trade negotiations, a high proportion of the benefits for Australia would come from reducing US import barriers on sugar and beef. When beef and sugar were later excluded in the course of negotiations, a new paper showed similar benefits but from a source that had been newly introduced into the analysis – the easing of conditions applied by the Foreign Investment Review Board to US investments. As a Senate Committee was advised, this did not pass the 'laugh test'.

During the debate on climate change policy, articles were published in the News Corp majority press by people with professional standing in economics who were at the same time principals of a consulting company that had undertaken lobbying work on the issues discussed in their articles. Readers were not informed of this conflict of interest.

The weakening of the authority of economic analysis and of economists' independence helped to increase the influence of populism and vested interests on policy-making. And because employment and income growth remained strong until 2011, the dismissal of economic analysis and productivity-raising and stability-enhancing reform seemed to have had no adverse consequences.

DID ECONOMISTS' MISTAKES DISCREDIT THEM?

Did mistakes in analysis contribute to the decline in the status of economics in policymaking? For the most part, reform worked much as economists had led political leaders and the public to expect. But the 1990–91 recession was the result of mistakes in monetary policy. In the early twenty-first century, the spending of the resources boom revenues more or less as they arrived was a mistake. It has left as a legacy the problems that are the subject of this book.

The deep recession of 1990–91 started the backlash against reform. It resulted from mistakes of two kinds. First, deregulation made it hard to measure monetary tightness by reference to old measures of money supply. This contributed to the policies that left too late both the raising of interest rates and their lowering as high rates placed great strain on the economy. The lesson from this experience was learned early and well: the rate of inflation is a better guide to changes in monetary policy than any measure of the growth rate of the money supply. The Reserve Bank adopted inflation targeting as its main guide to policy from the early 1990s.

The second source of error was tightening budget policy too little and monetary policy too much in the late-1980s boom. The idea of budget policy being too loose sounds strange when the Hawke government was running surpluses with as big a share of the economy as any before or since. Strange, but in retrospect true. This lesson has not yet been properly absorbed into economic thinking – as reflected in the general acceptance that the Howard surpluses in the bigger private-sector boom of the early 2000s were big enough.

Few in the community understood either of these issues. It was the recession itself that damaged the standing of economic analysis in policymaking.

HOW ELECTORAL DYNAMICS AFFECT POLICY

There is a Gresham's Law of electoral competition over policy. Bad policy ideas drive out the good. If one of the major parties offers something that is genuinely good for economic fortunes overall but which appears bad to part of the community, electoral fortunes can be won from fierce resistance to change.

There are several reasons for the electoral bias against reform in the public interest. Negative messages can be simple; reform and its consequences are usually not easy to explain in slogans. Simple messages have advantages in an electoral contest. The power of simple negative messages has been increased by changes in the media landscape since the Reform Era. The status quo is known, while reform inevitably carries uncertainty with it: 'Better the devil you know'; 'If you don't understand it, don't vote for it.'

Successful reforms in the public interest invariably hurt one or other vested interest. Those who are hurt know who they are. Ease of identification and concentration place the losers from reform in a good position to invest in opposition – to contribute to negative popular campaigns, to influence policy through campaign contributions, to finance the production and dissemination of misinformation.

The beneficiaries of reform are diffuse and harder to organise. The greatest beneficiaries may not be present at the time of reform, coming into existence only in response to the policy change.

In addition, the wider public is generally deeply resistant to the messages of mainstream economic analysis. It believes, or at least wishes, that trade protection increases employment and incomes. It will rarely see great strength in arguments for cutting spending now to reduce the risk of problems at a later date. It sees any immigration as reducing the chances of Australians finding and keeping a job.

For all of these reasons, reform in the public interest starts a long way behind in an electoral contest. It is only likely to succeed politically if there is effective advocacy of a clearly worked-out reform programme by a leader in a strong political position. The chances of success will be enhanced if a well-developed centre of the polity has absorbed influential people from both sides of the political contest (consensus being an unrealistic hope) who will increase the cost of appealing to populism by exposing the flaws in the simple arguments against reform.

The change in political culture between the Reform Era and the Great Complacency seems to throw up impossible barriers to far-reaching reform in the public interest. And yet the Reform Era is as much a historical reality as the Great Complacency. Australians now have large reason to return to the approaches to policy that underpinned the Reform Era.

CHAPTER 4
THE HAIR OF THE DOG

Australians now have to live with the hangover from the biggest housing, spending and resources booms in our boom-and-bust cluttered history. So far our response has been to take another drink, with no end in sight during the 2013 election campaign. Our spending and our real exchange rate have risen to levels far beyond what is sustainable. The challenge now is to manage their falls in ways that do the least damage to employment, our living standards and the quality of our society.

THE RESOURCES BOOM: THREE PHASES

As discussed in the Introduction, it is useful to think of three overlapping phases of the resources boom: the terms of trade phase, the investment phase and the export expansion phase. The terms of trade phase began in 2002 and affected the Australian economy from 2003. Apart from a break in the year following the Great Crash of

2008, our terms of trade rose rapidly and consistently to a peak in September 2011. The downward slide since then has been as rapid as the rise, and more likely than not in 2014 or 2015 we will see much lower levels still.

The investment phase got underway in 2006, but increased gradually until 2010 and also with a break after the Crash. Resources investment as a share of the economy looks set to reach a peak late in 2013. It will then decline until it is not far above the historical average in about 2017. The effect of this investment on the Australian economy in any year is a mixture of the positive, from the capital expenditure, and the negative, from the corporate tax deductions it allows. The net positive effect of resources investment was probably greatest in 2012 and will become a net negative for a number of years after 2017.

The third phase, the expansion in export volumes, began in 2012 and will continue for a year or so after the end of the investment phase, to about 2017.

If we put these three overlapping phases together, and since we spent most of the increased income from higher export prices as it arrived, we can see the expansionary effect of China's demand on the Australian economy commencing in 2003 and growing steadily stronger (with the break after the Great Crash) until 2011. The positive impact of the China resources boom on the overall Australian economy ended in late 2011. Since then, the overall impact of the resources sector has been contractive and is likely to remain so for a number of years.

The three phases contribute to the Australian economy in different ways. It is worth looking at each of them in more detail, so as to understand the underlying forces driving big changes in our economy.

THE BIGGEST PHASE: TERMS OF TRADE

Strong terms of trade contribute mainly to government revenue, but they also raise the income of Australians who own shares in resource companies. At their peak in September 2011, the terms of trade were more than double the average of the first twenty years of the floating currency (1983–2002). This added almost 24 per cent to *nominal* gross domestic product.

Yet much of this increase did not directly affect the Australian economy because about three-quarters of the equity in resource companies is owned overseas. The main effect of the higher terms of trade was to raise potential government revenue by around 10–11 per cent of GDP, with about 1 percentage point accruing to the states as royalties and the rest to the commonwealth as corporate income tax, capital gains tax, resource rent tax on offshore petroleum, income tax and withholding taxes on dividends from resource companies. (I say potential, because if the increased revenue is spent, as it was, it raises the cost level of the economy and the real exchange rate, which in turn reduces resource-sector profits and government revenue.)

Separately, the terms of trade raised potential Australian incomes by about 2.5–3 per cent of GDP through increased dividends or increases in the retained earnings of companies whose shares were held by Australians directly or within superannuation funds. There was an additional wealth effect as the price of resource company shares rose in anticipation of higher future earnings. So the total effect of the terms of trade boom from the average of 1983–2002 to the peak in late 2011 was to raise potential average incomes of Australians by more than one-eighth.

Since late 2011 there has been a steady decline in the resources sector's contribution to Australian incomes. How low will the terms of trade go and for how long? That depends on conditions specific to each industry.

For iron ore, immense investments in supply capacity in Australia and other countries are causing a huge increase in volumes to come to market at a time when the growth in Chinese demand has slowed sharply. This has brought down prices and will take them further as supplies increase considerably from late 2013. Similar dynamics are influencing metallurgical coal.

The extent of the reduction in Chinese production as prices fall will be an important determinant of future prices. There are prospects for average future iron ore and metallurgical coal prices to settle higher than in the late twentieth century, and lower-quality mines will come into production to meet absolutely higher levels of demand. But these prices may be only half the peaks of late 2011 in real terms. There could be early periods when China is undergoing structural change and global supply is increasing rapidly in which prices are temporarily lower than future averages.

Thermal coal use may not grow much, if at all, from late 2011 in China, the world's largest market, so that increasing global supplies may cause real prices to settle at much less than half the 2011 peaks. Again, much depends on what happens to production from mines in China.

Liquefied natural gas (LNG) exports will become increasingly important, so that gas prices will be influential in determining our terms of trade. Australian gas goes mainly to East Asia, where prices have been determined by formulae linked to oil and are now well above North American levels. Environmental priorities will cause Asian demand for gas to grow more strongly than for Australia's other commodity exports. At the same time, world capacity is growing rapidly, with big investments in exploration and production applying old as well as unconventional technologies. Large efforts to expand domestic gas supplies in China (not yet certain to have broad success), overland pipelines from central Asia and Russia, new supply capacity in Canada and Mexico (as ways are found to subvert US controls on gas exports), the relaxation of export restrictions from the United States and a huge expansion of seaborne export capacity in Australia, Papua New Guinea, Southeast Asia and the

Middle East are all increasing supplies to East Asia. The overall effects of these changes are not clear, but it would be surprising if Australian export prices didn't settle well below current levels in real terms.

Prices for tourism, education and other services are set in Australian dollars, so they rose for overseas customers as the real exchange rate went up, and will fall as the dollar comes down. This will place a significant drag on the terms of trade. Agricultural prices will generally be moderately higher than in the late twentieth century, reflecting Asian demand and constraints on global supplies.

My best guess is that the terms of trade will settle on average about a quarter higher than the 1983–2002 average, which is a bit more than one-quarter lower than mid-2013. Potential government revenue from resources would be about 7 per cent of GDP below the peak of 2011 (or about 4 per cent below mid-2013 levels). Other potential Australian incomes from ownership of shares in mining companies would contract by 2 per cent of GDP from the peak (or 1 per cent from mid-2013). This means that the 'permanent' contribution of the 21st-century lift in the terms of trade to Australians' average incomes is likely to amount to about 3 per cent of GDP, or about 10 percentage points lower than at the peak of the boom.

The increase in revenues from the boom could have been saved by government. If all of it *had* been saved, pending clarification of how much of the increase was going to be permanent, the main effect of the terms of trade boom would have been to support budget surpluses, mainly in the commonwealth but also in state governments.

As it turned out, almost all of the revenue increase was used for tax cuts or increased spending soon after it arrived. The resulting public and private spending increased the demand for Australian labour and supplies. The economy was already in full employment, so this in turn raised domestic costs and the real exchange rate. That forced the decline of other trade-exposed industries, which freed up the labour that had been employed in these industries. Every announcement of a new mine meant an unannounced closure or failure of a hotel or university department or winery or factory. This process continued until enough investment and production had been shrunk or closed to meet the demands that the higher expenditure was making.

The higher real exchange rate reduced the profitability of resources production (as well as of all other trade-exposed industries). It therefore took away part of the increase in government revenue. But this economic value did not just disappear – the real purchasing power of Australian incomes rose with cheaper imports, and Australian consumption increased to unprecedented levels.

Even with the higher exchange rate taking the edge off government revenues, the increase was remarkable. Corporate income tax receipts alone rose from $27 billion in 2002–03 to $65 billion in 2008–09. That was the high point in real terms: the revised budget numbers released in August 2013 showed that only $69 billion was expected in corporate tax revenue for 2013–14, which is one-eighth lower per Australian in real terms than five years before, in the midst of the global financial crisis.

THE INVESTMENT PHASE

The second phase of the resources boom saw capital expenditure on resources projects rise from historical averages of less than 2 per cent of GDP to more than 8 per cent in 2013. This investment contained a high proportion of imported goods and services, which reduced its impact on the Australian economy by perhaps a percentage point of GDP compared with the same amount of investment in other industries.

The big rise in investment began in 2006, stalled for a year or so after the Great Crash, and reached a peak in 2013. The larger part of the increase in resources investment came after the Great Crash.

Before the Great Crash, much of the increase was funded (directly or indirectly) by capital inflow. After the Crash, more was funded (mostly indirectly) from higher national savings. During this period, household savings increased, partly in response to the uncertainty and anxiety induced by the financial crisis and its long international shadow. Lower consumption reduced the demand for Australian labour, thereby freeing about half of what was required for the growth in mining investment from the Great Crash up to 2013. But the balance of the increase in investment – amounting to about 2 per cent of GDP – increased labour and other costs and therefore further pushed up the real exchange rate.

The investment phase of the boom has affected the economy independently of government decisions on taxation and expenditure. It immediately and automatically increased demand for Australian labour and supplies. This has augmented the effects of spending the income from higher export prices in pushing up local costs as mining outbid other industries.

The higher exchange rate made all of our trade-exposed industries less competitive – in the resources sector as well as in services, manufacturing and agriculture. So some of the investment choked off by the higher exchange rate was in resource projects that did not go ahead. Indeed, the bidding up of executive pay, labour costs and conditions, and land and materials prices in the frenzy of the boom meant that the resources sector experienced even greater cost increases in international dollars than other industries.

Once capital expenditures have been made, investors are able to claim tax deductions for depreciation and amortisation and financing costs. The increased deductions are available over a number of years, eventually accumulating to a 'loss' of revenue equal to about one-third of the increase in resources investment. So if the resources boom added an average of about 5 per cent of GDP to investment for eight years, it would lead to a reduction of commonwealth revenue of around 1–2 per cent of GDP per annum spread over perhaps ten years, but later.

These corporate tax deductions are available whether or not the investment is commercially successful. At the height of the boom, many investments were made that turned out to be commercially unsuccessful and were written off as worthless or written down in the accounts of the companies that made them. Some did not even lead to additional production. That happens in the ebullience of a boom.

THE EXPORT PHASE

The third phase of the resources boom – the lift in export volumes – began in earnest in 2012, almost a decade after the terms of trade began to rise. Exports in 2012 increased by 9 per cent for thermal coal, 18 per cent for metallurgical coal and 12 per cent for iron ore: the three main commodities contributing to the boom so far.

How much more will these exports grow? The Bureau of Resource Economics and Energy's September 2013 projections have been adjusted downwards from those presented at the height of the boom. They now anticipate growth in thermal coal exports of 43 per cent in the five years from 2012–13, and of 43 per cent for metallurgical coal and 59 per cent for iron ore. Even these lower projections of Australian exports (combined with large increases in other countries) would push prices down considerably now that China's import growth has eased.

Some established or new mines will be forced by the market to operate at well below design capacity. How much of the pull-back will be in Australia? That depends on competitiveness, which is weak with the exchange rate of mid-2013 and after the big exchange-rate falls in other resource-exporting countries, but a large real depreciation would change the story. The Bureau of Resources' estimates for Australian exports are now built on expectations of a further fall in the dollar to 86 US cents.

The Bureau's export projections for LNG show the largest increase: nearly 300 per cent, mostly between 2015 and 2018. This is possible given the Chinese government's encouragement of gas for environmental reasons, as well as the setback to nuclear energy in Japan caused by the Fukushima disaster.

These official forecasts are within the realm of the possible, after several years of being unrealistically high. There are still risks on the downside, especially if there is no large depreciation. The possibilities of surprise on the upside depend on a large real depreciation. Taking into account that iron ore, coal and LNG are not the whole of resources exports, and that resources are not the whole of exports, with the real exchange rate remaining at its mid-2013 level it is possible to envisage total export volumes rising by about 6 per cent per annum in the export expansion phase of the resources boom, between 2012–13 and 2017–18, with resources contributing almost the whole of the increase.

Only a modest proportion of this increase in resource export volumes contributes to the Australian economy. State government revenues grow relatively strongly, because their royalties depend on the value and not the profitability of exports. Higher volumes and moderately higher prices together will cause state revenues from resources to be larger by over 1 per cent of Australian GDP than before the boom. This revenue goes first to the export states, especially Western Australia and Queensland, but then is 'equalised' across the states and territories by our unique system of revenue distribution.

The commonwealth's revenue depends on profitability, and the new exports have much higher costs than the old. The commonwealth may receive less revenue from the increased export volumes than it loses from falls in price and increases in investment-related tax deductions until the early 2020s.

AVERAGE EMPLOYMENT IS ALREADY DECLINING

Spending the temporary bounty of the resources boom has caused the exchange rate to rise exceptionally. At its peak in early 2013, the real exchange rate was almost 70 per cent above the 1983–2003 average. The extent of the increase is unique in our history. Even after the substantial falls in the dollar in the second quarter of 2013, the real exchange rate was still one-half above that long-term average.

Such a lift caused other industries producing exports or competing against imports to contract. This is the phenomenon known as the 'Dutch Disease' or 'Gregory Effect'. The rapid increase in net exports in these industries as a share of the economy from the mid-1980s went into reverse, and by 2013 we were pretty well back where we had been before the Reform Era. Similarly, there was a switch from buying goods made in Australia to buying competing imports, and from producing goods and services for export to producing them for the home market.

If there is no adjustment of the real exchange rate and no budget stimulus (as discussed in Chapter 5), we can expect a smaller resources sector contribution to the economy in late 2017 than in 2013, which itself is lower than in 2011. The immediate impacts will lead to reductions in demand for other domestic goods and services, thereby magnifying the decline.

There has been a noticeable deceleration in the Australian economy since late 2011. Economic output has increased at less than long-term average rates and consistently below official estimates. Much of the decline has been felt as a fall in government revenue – with both commonwealth and state revenues consistently and steadily falling below estimates every six months since the second half of 2011. The main locus of the iron ore boom, the state of Western Australia, had its credit rating downgraded in September 2013. National employment grew less rapidly than the adult population, with monthly hours worked per adult falling from 89.1 to 86.8 between the peak in October 2011 and August 2013. Growth in real household income per adult has fallen from an average rate of around 2.5 per cent per annum in the decade to mid-2011 (a period without any productivity growth) to a third of that since then.

Australians continue to expect higher incomes, more services and lower taxes, but our economy's capacity to deliver these things to the average Australian is declining. In other words, Australia has been in the Dog Days since late 2011. Successive prime ministers and treasurers have been correct in saying that our economic conditions are among the best in the world. Yet Australian expectations of ever-increasing standards of living are now being disappointed.

Much of the public discussion about the end of the boom has so far focused on the unexpectedly large budget deficits since 2011. If the reaction of the government were simply to cut spending to match the fall in revenue, we would certainly enter a deep recession that would further reduce government revenues by a large amount. It is possible that the budget deficit would not be reduced at all by such spending cuts – it could even increase.

On the other hand, if we seek to maintain full employment with stimulus programmes, as in 2008–09, this will open up large budget and current account deficits. We could not fund this for long in current circumstances and would get ourselves into deep trouble if we tried.

This time, full employment has to be maintained with improvements in competitiveness: we have to switch demand from imports to goods and services produced in Australia; and switch production from the supply of home products to the supply of exports. This will primarily involve exporting Australian services, high-value manufactures and agriculture (probably mainly the adding of value to foodstuffs, as raw agricultural output is governed by weather in the short term). It can also include resource projects, such as processing, that would not have proceeded at the exchange rates of early 2013. Government policy choices and Australians' responses to them will have a large effect on how long and how far the fall in employment and living standards will extend. The best of policy will secure a large, early real fall in our currency as well as far-reaching productivity-raising reform.

But regardless of whether the large fall in the dollar comes sooner or later, if it is to have the necessary effect on the economy it must be converted into a real depreciation. This is the hard part. Australians on average will have to accept some reduction in real incomes. A 30 per cent fall in the exchange rate that is fully passed through into prices to consumers without any compensating increase in incomes would reduce average incomes by about 7–8 per cent.

A lower real exchange rate will restore competitiveness to all trade-exposed industries. It will take some time for this to lead to higher investment, and longer still for it to be reflected in higher exports.

NOTE: POLICY FOR STAYING FULLY EMPLOYED AND RICH

Some readers will not be interested in the economic analysis underlying the policy choices that I discuss in the next part of the book, so I separate that out here so that those who are comfortable about taking my analytic framework on faith can proceed directly to the next chapter.

The economic challenge facing Australia has two parts: keeping our people fully employed without inflation or dislocations in external payments (at worst, a financial crisis); and doing things efficiently so that we achieve full employment with the highest possible standards of living for ordinary Australians.

The first part of the challenge is macro-economic: the big economic picture of achieving full employment without inflation by maintaining a balance between overall income and expenditure, and foreign income and foreign expenditure. The second is micro-economic: achieving high productivity in the market sector and effectiveness of government.

Chapter 5 outlines the first part of the challenge, the macro-economic. Chapters 6, 7 and 8 deal with what we can do to increase standards of living sustainably, the micro-economic.

Macro-economics can be as complex as we want to make it. Its essence is simple, so let's make it simple. For economic growth to proceed smoothly with full employment and without unacceptably high inflation, we need to keep a balance in two areas: between total expenditure and the economy's capacity to generate income; and between expenditure now and expenditure in the future.

We have two policy objectives: maintaining full employment and low inflation now; and avoiding big external payments imbalances so that we don't store up potential for financial crises and employment and inflation problems.

We have main two levers to pull on the way to achieving these objectives. One is to vary the budget deficit or surplus by changing the level of government expenditure or taxation. The other is to vary the interest rate in order to vary the exchange rate and therefore the relative level of domestic and foreign costs. Changing the interest rate also affects expenditure, which augments or counteracts changes in the budget settings.

The balance between expenditure and income ensures that there is enough demand to generate full employment, but not so much as to give rise to inflation. If this were our only concern, it would not matter whether we controlled demand by changing the budget deficit or surplus, or the interest rate. If demand were too low, we could lower interest rates to lower the dollar and increase demand, or run a bigger budget deficit. It would not matter which.

But the balance between demand and incomes today is not all that matters. If incomes exceed expenditure now – perhaps because the private sector has decided to save more than it invests – we will have a tendency to unemployment. If we fill the demand gap simply by increasing budget expenditure or cutting taxes without lowering interest rates (and therefore the exchange rate), the trade deficit will increase. That is fine if our external financial position is strong and expected to remain so through an increase in the trade deficit. But it is not fine if the external financial position is weak and expected to get weaker.

If we lower interest rates, there will be some increase in domestic expenditure. In addition, the exchange rate will fall – and some of the increase in employment will come from the export- and import-competing industries. The trade balance will be stronger than it would have been if expansion had come only through the budget.

If the terms of trade increase, Australian incomes rise. If we start from a position of full employment and all of the extra income is spent, we will have a tendency to inflation. The appropriate response is to reduce spending. We can do that through running a budget surplus and sterilising it by investing it abroad, or through raising interest rates and therefore the exchange rate. There are two big differences between the two cases. One is that current average Australian incomes rise if the tightening occurs through the exchange rate, but not otherwise. The other is that the cutback in expenditure is spread through government and other non-traded activities with the budget tightening, but disproportionately concentrated in the export- and import-competing industries if it is achieved through higher interest rates. The more we force the cutback on the trade-exposed industries, the larger the trade deficit and increase in foreign debt, and the more we redistribute real incomes and consumption from future to current generations.

Which is better? It all depends. It depends first of all on whether the change that has increased our incomes is expected to be temporary or permanent. If temporary, it will be disruptive if we let real incomes and expenditure rise, and force other trade-exposed industries to reduce their investment and production, and then have to pull them down again when things return to where they were. And we can feel more comfortable about redistributing income away from future and towards current generations if seemingly permanent high terms of trade are going to make future Australians well off.

You never know for sure whether and how much of a change in export prices is going to be temporary. It is a costly error to assume that a lift in export prices is permanent when it turns out to be temporary: to spend the increased incomes and then have to manage down the excessively high incomes, expenditures and real exchange rate. It is much less costly to make the opposite error: to assume that the increase is temporary when it turns out to be permanent. It is therefore wise to be cautious and respond initially to a positive shock with a tighter budget.

I should add another complication in choosing whether to increase the budget deficit or reduce interest rates when we need to increase expenditure and employment. Lower interest rates stimulate expenditure directly as well as lower the exchange rate, and on some activities much more than on others. Housing expenditure is particularly sensitive to interest rates. Worries about a housing bubble may eventually inhibit the Reserve Bank's cutting of interest rates when this is warranted on other grounds. In these circumstances, the authorities may need to apply special measures to slow the growth in lending for housing as interest rates are cut lower.

If required, the most straightforward way of restraining house prices as interest rates are reduced is to decrease or remove the unusually low proportion of housing loans that the Australian Prudential Regulatory Authority requires banks to put aside for capital adequacy purposes. The reason why capital adequacy requirements are low is that housing loans are thought to be less risky. This justification falls away when the rise in housing prices has made lending risky.

The best mixture of budget and interest rate policies needs to be worked out case by case. Let's look at how this has occurred through the China resources boom, so we can understand better what to do next.

We started with full employment and a bit of a tendency towards over-expenditure in the housing and consumption boom. We spent the extra government revenue and private income just about as soon as we received it. The Reserve Bank raised interest rates and the exchange rate rose. This choked off investment and export growth in other export- and import-competing industries – and the more marginal resource projects themselves. Real Australian incomes and expenditure rose. (I'll leave the years of the Great Crash out of this story, as they are an unnecessary complication.)

When resources investment started to rise strongly, financed partly from new capital inflow and partly from domestic savings (some of which were diverted from non-resource investments that were not now happening), the Reserve Bank further increased interest rates in order to ensure that the extra demand for labour and materials was not inflationary. The fact that other developed countries' interest rates were being kept close to zero as they tried to encourage growth after the financial crisis meant that our exchange rate went higher still, as it is the difference between Australian and foreign interest rates that drives the foreign exchange value of our dollar.

And then something unusual happened. The central banks of the large developed countries wanted to stimulate economic activity even more, and started pushing more cash into their economies. That drove down their currencies even further – which amounted to driving up the currencies of economies that did not follow such policies. Some foreign central banks that did not engage in the unconventional monetary policy, including the Swiss and Brazilian, resisted the increase in value of their own currencies by intervening in the foreign exchange market in various ways. That made the lift in the exchange rate even bigger for those currencies that did not intervene in any way – Australia foremost among them.

So by March 2013 we were in the position described in Part 1 of the book, with a real exchange rate that has appreciated more than any developed country's currency ever had, with our terms of trade on the way down, and our resources investment at its peak and about to go down. Export volumes are growing strongly, but total exports not especially so; certainly not enough to fill the gap in economic activity left by retreating terms-of-trade-based expenditures and resource investment. That is the reality that will shape Australian policy choice in the period ahead.

This simple story raises a question about why the official advisers to the government did not push Prime Minister Howard and Treasurer Costello much harder towards budget surplus in the early years of the boom.

Part of the reason was that the wrong lesson was learned about the importance of the mix of fiscal and monetary policy from the boom of the late 1980s and applied in the China resources boom. The Hawke government in the late 1980s ran just about the tightest budget policy in Australian history – as measured by the budget surplus as a share of GDP. Tight, but not tight enough to avoid the emergence of an inflationary boom. The lesson drawn was that the budget instrument was ineffective. In retrospect, the correct lesson was that surpluses were not big enough.

There was another source of error in managing the early stages of the resources boom. There has been overconfidence that the reformed economy will adjust automatically to changes in the terms of trade if large public deficits are avoided, and interest rates are raised when inflation is high and lowered when unemployment is emerging. We will all learn over the next few years whether the downward adjustment of real incomes, expenditure and the real exchange rate turns out to be hard or easy. I fear that it will be hard.

Finally, policymakers early in the resources boom may have thought that developments in China meant that the increase in the terms of trade was likely to be permanent – that this time was different. If so, this was an imprudent assessment.

Figure 1: Monthly hours worked (three monthly averages) per person over fifteen years

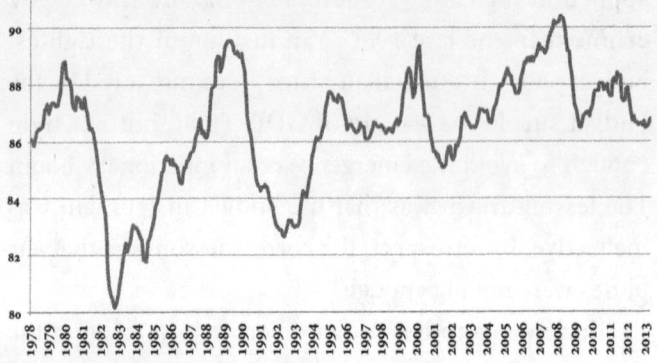

Source: Australian Bureau of Statistics

Figure 2: From Champagne to Coonawarra and back to Champagne

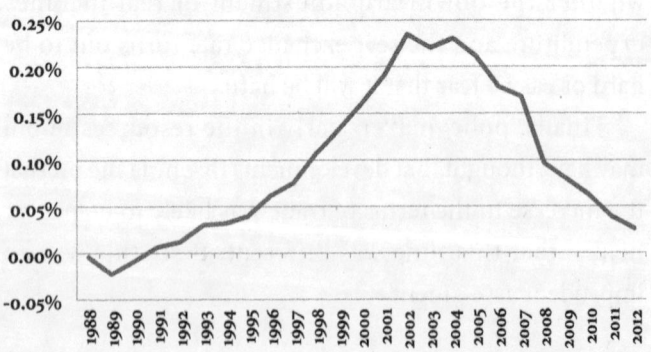

Source: Australian Bureau of Statistics

Figure 3: Tourism levels: arrivals as a proportion of departures (rolling annual)

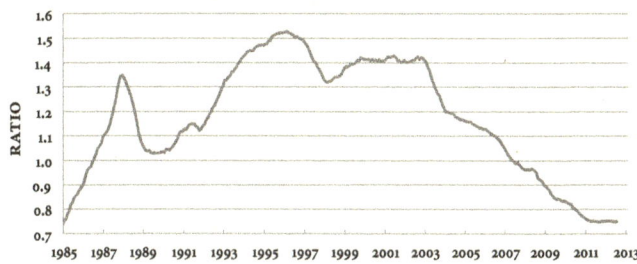

Source: Australian Bureau of Statistics

Figure 4. The real exchange rate of the Australian dollar (TWI)

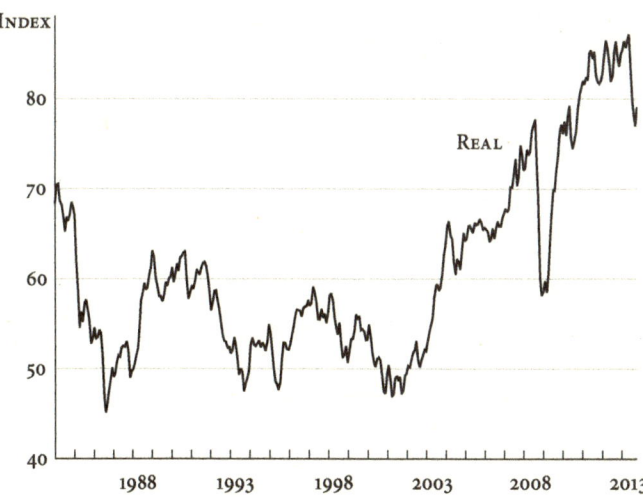

Sources: ABS; RBA; Thomson Reuters; WM/Reuters

FIGURE 5: TERMS OF TRADE*

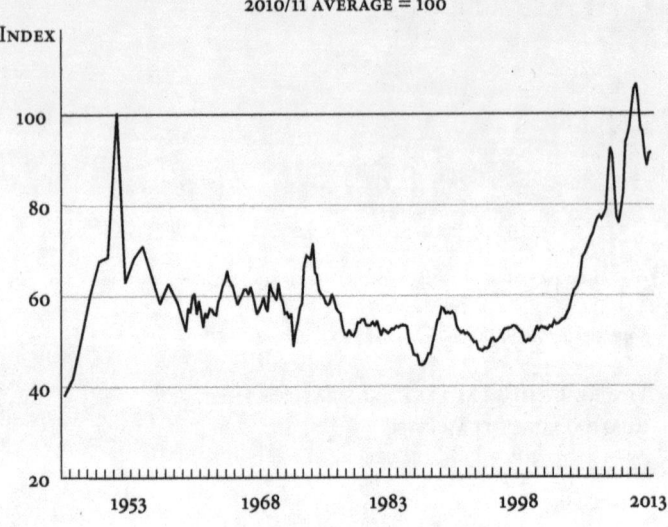

* ANNUAL DATA ARE USED PRIOR TO 1960

Sources: ABS; RBA

PART 2

CHAPTER 5
REFORM FOR FULL EMPLOYMENT AND STABILITY

This chapter examines more closely the big economic policy adjustment that Australia must make if it is to maintain full employment and a base for rising prosperity after the China resources boom.

When the China boom has passed completely into history, it will have left us with a bit more spending power than before it began. But for a while we will have much less spending power than we were enjoying at the height of the boom in 2011, less than we are enjoying as this book goes to print in 2013, and much, much less than Australians came to expect as the normal accompaniment to life in the Salad Days.

This is not the conventional wisdom in the business community and much of the media, which expects a return to comfortable times as 'confidence' returns with the end of minority government and the blossoming of resource exports from now on.

Yet Australian employment and incomes face strong headwinds. Among the long-term factors, whatever the permanent increase in incomes from the boom in the resources sector, there will be more Australians to share it. The ageing of the population is beginning to bite, with rising health and aged-care costs; and the increase in the number of dependents supported by each working-age Australian will reduce average incomes by about 0.25 per cent annually for as far ahead as we can see.

Our economy has high levels of foreign debt as a share of the economy – overwhelmingly in the private sector. At some time, international interest rates will rise and the servicing of this debt will be an increased drag on incomes. While the debt is mostly private, commonwealth tax revenue will be affected by higher deductions as interest rates rise.

Climate change is affecting economic growth. The world has been slow to reduce emissions and the cost of dealing with climate change will increase in the years ahead, even in the best of circumstances. Much change is locked in by emissions that are already in the atmosphere or impossible to avoid. For Australia to do its fair share in the global effort to reduce emissions – and therefore reduce future costs of climate change – also has a cost. The lowest-cost approaches to mitigation involving carbon pricing would shave a tenth of a percentage point off incomes growth per annum in the years immediately ahead; direct interventions would cost much more to meet the same targets.

Average productivity growth in all developed countries has been much lower so far in the twenty-first than in the twentieth century. This makes it harder to achieve strong productivity growth in Australia. Of course, we can raise productivity significantly simply by moving closer to the best ways of doing things in other countries. That would help us to retain some of the increase in living standards that has accrued during the Great Complacency. But we are yet to start on a vigorous programme of productivity-raising reform.

As noted, no developed country has experienced as large a sustained appreciation in its real exchange rate as Australia has through the China resources boom – not even the Netherlands during the development of North Sea gas and the fabled 'Dutch Disease'. In turn, this means that no developed country has ever successfully worked through such a fall in the real exchange rate and associated contraction of incomes.

HOLES IN THE GREAT COMPLACENCY

In short, Australian economic policy and experience has entered unknown territory. The decline from the peak of the China resources boom in late 2011 wasn't noticed much at first. From 2010 I had started to draw attention to new currents in China and point out the implications for Australia, but this wasn't the time for these matters to be noticed.

Larger holes began to appear in the Great Australian Complacency from early 2013. Discussion of policy alternatives became possible. The then prime minister, Kevin Rudd, talked about the transition after the end of the boom on the day of his return to office in June 2013. For his part, the then treasurer, Chris Bowen, said in his August Economic Statement, delivered just before the 2013 election was called, that we are in a transition and not a crisis. If this means that we treat the policy choices purposefully and systematically, without panic, then he struck the right note. If it conveys the idea that small, incremental adjustments can solve the problem, then it was unfortunate.

Levels of commonwealth spending and revenue were the prime focus of the government's August statement on the budget and economic outlook, the Opposition's response and the arguments of the election campaign. However, in the adjustment to the end of the boom, Australia faces an *economic* problem, of which the budget problem is a part. The budget problem will be solved in the process of solving the economic problem, or not at all. In any case, if budgetary extravagance was the problem, the tightest budget in at least sixty years would have been a reasonable start on a solution.

It is the competitiveness of Australia's trade-exposed industries, not the state of the budget in the years immediately ahead, that will determine whether we can restore and maintain full employment. The size of the budget deficit matters much more than the post-election public conversation allows; but the extent of future deficits and their consequences depends crucially on whether or not Australia succeeds in real depreciation and restoring momentum to our export- and import-competing industries.

FIVE APPROACHES TO RESTORING FULL EMPLOYMENT AND GROWTH

We can identify five approaches to the economic challenge facing Australia: 'business as usual', 'austerity', 'budget stimulus', 'productivity growth' and 'real depreciation'. Any effective strategy will contain elements of more than one of these approaches, but it helps our understanding to separate them out.

Business as Usual

'Business as usual' is a continuation of what the authorities were doing from the time that the resources boom passed its peak in 2011 up to the middle of 2013. Budget policy is firm, with historically low real growth in expenditure. Taxation rates are presumed to stay as they are. On the assumption that growth soon resumes and continues at a bit above 3 per cent per annum, it is projected that the budget is back in balance in two to three years. Interest rates are reduced when economic growth is well below trend, the labour market is weak and inflation is in the target band of 2–3 per cent.

The presumption is that good times will return before too long; programmes to increase expenditure are introduced, so long as they have their main impact beyond the four years of the forward budget estimates.

Every six months there are new official forward estimates. Each of these since late 2011 has involved a large downward revision of revenue – for the current year and the several years beyond.

This puzzles official and most private analysts when the data first comes in. Then it is realised that the weak revenues are the result of economic growth being slower than expected, employment weaker than expected, average incomes lower than expected, inflation lower than expected. Company income tax is far lower than expected partly because incomes are lower for all of the above reasons, partly because export prices are low, and especially because the estimates greatly underestimate the size of the tax deductions attached to the resources investment boom. (The huge write-downs in estimates of revenue in the May 2013 budget and the August 2013 revisions mainly reflected receipts from company income tax and resource rent tax falling below expectations.)

Under the old 'business as usual', the Labor government made firm and unqualified commitments to securing a budget surplus a couple of years into the future. So, as disappointingly low revenue from a weakening economy showed up in the accounts, six-monthly statement after six-monthly statement, the government responded by announcing tax increases and spending cuts that would have their main effect in the later years of the four-year projections. The budget deficit was always a bit bigger than had been expected, and the return to surplus always remained about as far into the future as it had been when the resources boom started to recede.

There are Labor and Coalition versions of 'business as usual'. Rhetorically, the Labor government was more cautious about cutting spending than the Coalition. However, in practice the Abbott Coalition government has accepted nearly all of the former government's spending commitments, rejected some of its proposals for increased taxation, and added some tax cuts and expenditure increases of its own.

The new government's promises to remove and reduce tax add up to a large unacknowledged long-term expansion of the 'business as usual' budget deficit. These promises – to remove carbon pricing and the Minerals Resource Rent Tax (MRRT), and to reduce the company tax rate and the fringe benefits tax on private motor vehicle use – all have increasing revenue effects over time, with their sum much greater beyond the four-year estimates.

Under 'business as usual', monetary policy is varied if inflation rates tend higher or lower than 2–3 per cent and the economy is unusually strong or weak. The exchange rate is left to find its own level. If other countries follow unusually expansive monetary policies (even as their real output growth per person comes to exceed Australia's, as it has recently in Japan and the United States), we accept the higher exchange rate flowing from that. We also accept the higher exchange rate that comes from the central banks of other countries deciding for the first time to hold large amounts of Australian dollars (almost $100 billion to June 2013 by countries other than China and an unknown but large sum by the People's Bank of China). We accept the loss of competitiveness that comes from rival resource suppliers artificially securing large reductions in their own exchange rates. Interest rates are lowered only after weakness in the economy and low inflation becomes apparent. This means the exchange rate will eventually fall, but may remain uneconomically high for a long period.

The Reserve Bank of Australia has been lowering interest rates behind the weakening economy since November 2011, so that by August 2013 the 'cash rate' reductions amounted to 2.25 per cent and the official rate was lower than it had ever been. The lower interest rates helped to bring down the exchange rate from early May 2013, but – because of the exceptional nature of monetary policy in larger developed economies – not by as much as might have been expected. The exchange-rate fall was partially reversed in early September when it became clear that the exceptional monetary expansion of the United States would continue for the time being.

In sum, the increase in activity from interest rate and exchange rate falls so far is helpful but too small to counteract the powerful contraction set in train by the decline in the resources sector's contribution to the economy. The slow growth and deterioration in employment can be expected not only to continue, but also to feed on themselves. Economic weakness and lower interest rates will eventually see further falls in the Australian dollar.

The Treasury's and Reserve Bank's projections envisage a return to normal rates of growth of around 3 per cent per annum and of normal unemployment at about 5 per cent from 2015–16. In the forward estimates, stronger economic growth painlessly removes unemployment and the budget deficit. The forward estimates assume continuation of the exchange rate at the time they were prepared – the latest a few cents below the mid-September level. But what will generate new investment and other domestic spending under these settings as resources investment shrinks? What will generate the increased economic activity that re-establishes full employment and public revenue growth without a large fall in the real exchange rate?

Without real depreciation of the currency, it won't be investment in the resources industries. It won't be investment in the other export industries. It won't be government expenditure under current budget settings. It won't be consumption: household income is growing at historically low rates and there is no sign of a lower rate of savings.

There will be a contribution from increased resources exports, but this will not do much for economic activity or jobs. There will be a contribution from housing under the influence of low interest rates, but that will need to be monitored for the emergence of a bubble, and in any case it cannot carry the whole economy without creating risks in the external accounts.

'Business as usual' would be a good strategy if there were a reasonable chance of a return to trend rates of economic growth, low unemployment and budget surplus by 2016–17 without external payments pressures emerging. Regrettably, the Treasury and Reserve Bank projections are a clock face in which the hands have been moved to a new time without a locomotive mechanism.

It seems more likely that 'business as usual' will lead to a continuing deterioration in economic activity, employment and the public finances, at least through the four years covered by the forward estimates. In the absence of a large currency depreciation, I expect the budget deficit for 2015–16 and 2016–17 will be many billions of dollars larger than projected in the treasurer's Statement of August 2013. Meanwhile, the new Coalition government's highest-profile commitments worsen the budget problem beyond the four years and increase the challenge of making the required adjustments equitably. At the same time, none of its high-profile policy changes is structured to have a large positive effect on economic activity.

Austerity

The 'austerity' approach involves discretionary increases in taxation and structural spending cuts in an attempt to balance the budget quickly. The former Labor government's final economic and financial statements suggested that it would return the budget to surplus by 2016–17. Its practice in government had been to take steps in that direction and then to let the deficit stay high if revenue was disappointingly low. The new government hasn't committed itself even nominally to a surplus in 2016–17. Its rejection of austerity is appropriate under the circumstances.

One can envisage forward-looking as well as immediate approaches to austerity – the former would focus on cutting back programmes that affect the structural deficit only in future years; the latter on early expenditures and tax rates.

Under austerity, economic activity would be weaker in the short to medium term. Budget revenues would fall further. Recession in the near term would be likely. This could then lead to a shift towards a 'real depreciation' approach, but maybe only after a long period of economic underperformance.

Budget Stimulus

Using the budget to stimulate the economy in the face of recession would involve large, early measures to stoke domestic demand. It would see the government respond to a deteriorating economy and rising unemployment with a version of the policies adopted in response to the Great Crash of 2008: increased commonwealth expenditure, and probably some tax cuts. The reduction of interest rates would be lessened and therefore would do less to lower the exchange rate if accompanied by an expansion of the budget deficit. A bigger budget deficit from stimulus would be counteracted to some extent by higher government revenue from the increased economic activity. So why not do it?

The binding constraint is Australia's external accounts over the longer term. If we seek to return to full employment through greater spending – whether public through the budget or private through low interest rates – but without a large real depreciation, sooner or later the current account deficit and foreign debt as a share of the economy will blow out to unsustainable levels.

There are two good reasons to be cautious about an approach that requires increased foreign debt. First, average Australian spending and incomes are higher now than they are likely to be for a number of years. Increased debt would have to be repaid by future generations who may not be as well off as ourselves, still warmed as we are by the embers of the resources boom.

Second, our immediate external financial position is weaker now, after the peak of the China resources boom, than it was following the Great Crash. If we seek to restore full employment over the next few years simply by increasing spending, with no sustained improvement in international competitiveness, the current account deficit will rise to an unusual and risky proportion of GDP. This deficit was over 3 per cent of GDP in the first nine months of 2012–13: not exceptionally high by recent Australian standards, but uncomfortably large given likely developments in the years immediately ahead. The increased spending to return the economy to full employment will increase imports, while the large corporate tax deductions from the investment phase of the resources boom will be mostly paid out to overseas owners or lenders. Furthermore, the normalisation of global interest rates after their fall following the Great Crash will increase the costs of servicing Australia's external debt and add 1 to 2 per cent of GDP to external payments. The net external-payments effect of the reduced resource investment and the increased expenditure that takes its place will cancel each other out. Total export volumes are unlikely to rise fast enough to offset the negative effects, especially since only a modest proportion of export receipts stay within the domestic economy.

Under these circumstances, Australia will have to finance a current account deficit that is high by historical and global experience, at a time of economic underperformance and when our international halo from the China boom is fading. There will be no prospect of doing this for long without increased costs of debt and without doubts arising about our capacity to service it. These factors will have their own negative effects on the economy.

This perspective contradicts an alternative view that still has considerable support in Australia: that the growth in export volumes during the production phase of the resources boom will solve our external payments and growth problems. There is nothing especially advantageous about mining over other exports unless prices are high enough to generate large economic rents that are collected for the public revenues. To the contrary, the high foreign components of resources production mean that the domestic contribution per dollar of exports is somewhat smaller than that of services, agricultural and manufactures exports.

As noted, the large increase in resource exports, especially after 2011, has been offset by the cessation of growth in other exports. And while the total volume of Australian exports can be expected to grow as new resource projects come on-stream over the next half a dozen years (perhaps by about 6 per cent per annum), this will not be an unusually high rate – not, for instance, as high as the average in the seventeen years of the Reform Era. It's not an export boom in historical context.

A variation on the stimulus theme suggests that we increase domestic economic activity by government investment in productivity-raising infrastructure. The treasurer, Joe Hockey, has suggested that investment in infrastructure be increased to offset the decline in activity associated with the fall in resources investment. This is different from increased government consumption expenditure to the extent that the investment will lead to higher productivity growth in the economy as a whole than would otherwise be the case. If this condition is met, increased borrowing (and the extra will be foreign borrowing) will be a bit easier to secure on reasonable terms, in turn making it easier for future Australians to repay. It is more reasonable for contemporary Australians to ask their successors to service a debt if it arises from expenditure that gives them an improved standard of living.

For us to have confidence that such an investment will be genuinely productivity-raising for the economy as a whole, it will need to have been subject to independent, transparent and rigorous cost-benefit analysis and full engineering design in advance of the need for it. Keynes suggested in his General Theory that public works were especially valuable in boosting expenditure in a downturn, and elsewhere suggested that governments should keep proposals for such works ready to go. Early post-war Australian governments followed this wise practice.

The stimulus strategy involves a bigger budget deficit and by implication higher interest and exchange rates for any given level of domestic expenditure. This is what distinguishes it from real depreciation. It is associated with lower levels of investment and production in the trade-exposed industries – and this is reflected in greater exposure to the exigencies of external financial markets.

Productivity Growth

'Productivity growth' recognises that increasing productivity is the only sustainable source of continuously rising living standards. It focuses on reversing the decline in productivity growth over the Great Australian Complacency.

The early 21st-century slump in growth productivity has been larger in Australia than in most developed countries. A comparison with other resource-rich developed countries is perhaps more relevant. The decline in productivity from 2006 to 2010 was identical in Canada and Australia (1.1 per cent per annum). However, productivity growth remained positive in the other resource-rich developed country, Norway, with its incomparably different approach to collecting resource rents for the public revenue and saving them for future use.

There is rich potential for gains from reform. However, reform to increase productivity can play only a supporting role in the early years, because there are speed limits to productivity growth. At the high point in the harvest years of the Reform Era in the 1990s, productivity was rising at 2.5 per cent per annum. That is as high as can reasonably be expected in modern times. Australia would be doing extremely well if its productivity growth were one percentage point above the average of other developed countries. But even with such stellar performance, it would take decades for us to achieve the required improvement in competitiveness through productivity growth alone.

Real Depreciation

This approach places priority on a lower exchange rate for the dollar, and converting this into a real depreciation.

How low is low enough? The real exchange rate will have to fall enough to induce enough investment in other export industries to fill the hole left by the decline in the resources sector. The market will sort out how large the depreciation needs to be: when we see the investor response to a lower dollar, it will be clear whether or not the exchange rate needs to fall further. At the end of the 2013 March quarter, when the Australian dollar was valued at $US1.05, I expressed the view that a real depreciation in the range of 20–40 per cent would be required to maintain high levels of employment with a sustainable current account deficit. This would mean a value of 63–84 US cents.

How can we secure the rest of the necessary devaluation? Interest rate cuts in May and the anticipation of more contributed to a fall in the dollar. By June, the effects of lower interest rates on the dollar were being supported rhetorically by the prime minister, other senior ministers, and senior officers of the Reserve Bank and the Treasury. This contrasted with the defence of a high dollar from some of these officials early in the year.

The restored prime minister, Kevin Rudd, initially made adjustment to the end of the China resources boom the central element in a renewed focus on economic reform, but this became simply rhetorical once the election was called for early September. By then, the dollar had fallen by about 10 per cent against major currencies – around half of the minimum fall that I had suggested.

Weakness in the economy and the reductions in interest rates that follow under 'business as usual' will eventually bring down the dollar by a large amount. But there is a large difference between a fall in the dollar that happens in *response* to economic weakness and one that happens in *anticipation* of it. This can be the difference between recession accompanied by high unemployment, and a moderate economic downturn.

We will learn through 2014 and afterwards whether the lowering of interest rates and fall in the dollar were too little, too late to avoid a major dislocation in Australian prosperity. But even if it turns out that we are too late to avoid uncomfortably high unemployment, the downturn will be less severe and end sooner if the exchange rate falls earlier rather than later and more rather than less, and if policy and community responses turn the fall into a real depreciation.

How can we get an earlier rather than later depreciation in the exchange rate?

More interest rate cuts are the first step. This is easy to justify while the economy is growing slowly and employment per person falling, as they have been through 2013. The cuts will be more effective if clear messages are put out by the Reserve Bank and the new government that a fall in the dollar is welcome. This reduces the risk in the minds of people investing in a lower dollar that the authorities may take action to prevent the dollar from falling. As discussed in the Note at the end of Chapter 4, it may be necessary to adopt prudential measures to constrain risky lending for housing as interest rates fall.

Will the weakening economy, the easing of interest rates and official rhetoric take the dollar low enough, soon enough? The answer depends partly on what happens in other countries. A return to reasonably strong economic growth and more normal monetary policies in Europe, Japan and the United States would raise their exchange rates against Australia. At some point, the realisation that the Australian dollar is likely soon to fall by a large amount would reduce its attraction as a reserve currency. Otherwise, intervention along the lines of that taken by the Swiss central bank should be contemplated if lower interest rates, official rhetoric and monetary policy changes in other countries do not do the job.

The Reserve Bank needs to be concerned about the inflationary effects of lower interest rates. But it is not the Bank's only responsibility. Here there is a governance issue that has been discussed less than its importance warrants. The law under which the Reserve Bank operates requires it to give at least as much priority to full employment as to inflation. The Reserve Bank since 1996 has operated within instructions from the Australian treasurer to hold inflation within the range 2–3 per cent. The Bank would be in breach of the law if it acted on an instruction from a member of the Executive that was in conflict with an Act of the Parliament. (Seeking to do just this cost Charles I his head.)

In any case, the Bank has been prepared to overlook temporary inflation deriving from a large fall in the exchange rate. It did this during the Asian Financial Crisis.

TURNING A LOW DOLLAR INTO A REAL DEPRECIATION

A 20–40 per cent fall in the foreign exchange rate without any pass-through into domestic costs and prices reduces the real incomes of many people and firms. Turning a nominal into a real depreciation is the most difficult part of a successful adjustment to the end of the boom. If the exchange rate falls without strong leadership from government to avoid the pass-through of costs, there is likely to be a drift into continuing inflation and rising unemployment.

Monopoly pricing, which has denied Australian consumers the full benefits of the dollar's rise by holding prices for imported goods and services well above those in other countries, may have an opposite effect on the dollar's way down. Suppliers of imported and other goods and services who expanded profit margins when the dollar was strong may allow their compression as the dollar weakens. Evidence from earlier, smaller and less durable depreciations suggests that at least a few per cent of real depreciation may be achievable through these mechanisms without a fall in the standard of living of ordinary Australians. Otherwise, it is the task of leaders to explain that restraint to avoid the pass-through into domestic costs of an increase in prices of imports and exportable goods and services is in the interests of nearly all Australians. This is more likely to be successful as part of a programme of wider reform aiming at securing sustainable prosperity.

EARNING OUR LUCK IN THE ASIAN CENTURY

The old model of China's growth greatly increased demand for a few resource products that Australia was uniquely well placed to supply. Continued strong growth, particularly in China, but also India, Indonesia and much of the rest of developing Asia, will expand our opportunities for exports from non-resource industries, as well as place a historically high floor under some of the mineral and energy commodities that were at the centre of the China boom.

New opportunities for the expansion of Australia's exports to Asia include processed foodstuffs, specialised manufactures, and services in education, tourism, engineering, business, architecture, law and medicine. For all of these exports, our relative proximity to international markets confers advantages. For services, our location within similar time zones to Asia confers special advantages over the developed countries that are our main competitors.

However, Australia's advantages for the new export industries are not unique and overwhelming as they are in iron ore, coal and, for the time being, natural gas.

Australian suppliers of non-resource goods and services will be engaged in intense competition with exporters in developed countries all over the world, countries whose competitiveness has been honed by hard times since the Great Crash of 2008.

It is a great advantage that we are well placed to make use of new opportunities in the Asian Century after the China resources boom. But from now on we will have to earn our luck.

A SUCCESSFUL STRATEGY BASED ON REAL DEPRECIATION

A strategy to restore full employment with the highest possible living standards contains the following elements.

First, interest rates are reduced until the dollar has fallen enough to rekindle investment in the export- and import-competing industries. Special measures may need to be taken to prevent low interest rates from leading to inflation in housing if this is seen to be rising imprudently. Other measures are considered if the exchange rate stays high.

Second, the government seeks broad public support for conversion of the fall of the dollar into a real depreciation. This will require steps to ensure that the burden of adjustment is shared fairly.

Third, the government stimulates the economy by investment in productive infrastructure.

Fourth, a programme of uninhibited productivity-raising reform is developed, as discussed in the next two chapters.

CHAPTER 6
REFORM TO RAISE PRODUCTIVITY

Productivity relates to the amount of economic value generated from a given amount of labour and capital. Productivity as conventionally measured only makes sense for the production of goods and services exchanged in markets. The ownership of producers can be public or private so long as the goods and services are exchanged and given a value in the market. Productivity, in this sense, relates to about two-thirds of today's Australian economy.

The American economist Paul Krugman famously said that productivity isn't everything, but in the long run it's almost everything. But the short and medium run also matter, and in these timeframes participation in the labour force has quite a lot to do with whether average incomes rise or fall. We add significantly to average incomes if we encourage Australians into the labour force and then allow them to have as much paid work as they prefer to do. Participation affects economic output but not productivity as conventionally measured. The employment of more people for more hours enhances output, welfare and equity. Yet it may reduce productivity, since it may increase the labour supply by proportionately more than it increases output – as it did when workforce participation grew rapidly in the 1980s. (I discuss participation in Chapter 7.)

The idea of productivity can be applied to non-market services within the public sector. However, there is a danger that any particular measure of value for these services provided by government will be arbitrary, contentious and liable over time to give a false sense of precision. I prefer to talk about the *effectiveness* of the public sector, so that we are not pretending that we are dealing with anything precise. (Effectiveness of government is the focus of Chapter 8.)

I use the term 'living standards' many times in this book. I am only referring to the consumption of material goods and services. It should go without saying – but sometimes needs saying – that material living standards are not the only determinants of human welfare.

When I talk about achieving full employment with the highest possible standard of living, I am referring to a standard that is sustainable in future – a standard enjoyed by Australians now that can also be provided for those in the future. Adjustments to lower standards of living are difficult, painful and disruptive. When we think about it, not many of us are comfortable about enjoying a level of consumption of goods and services that cannot be passed on to those who follow us – in the next decade or the next generation or the generation after that. People living at one time can always consume more goods and services than will be available to those who come after them by running up high levels of private and public debt (which is especially difficult for the future if it's funded by foreigners), or weakening the institutions upon which our civilisation depends, or damaging irreparably the natural environment. But when we see that we are living unsustainably, the decisions that allowed it are invariably regarded as a mistake, resulting from a lack of information or failure of analysis or failure of our political system to make choices that reflect the underlying preferences of most Australians.

The difficult adjustment that we are facing now is actually an example of Australians at one point in time – those living through the China resources boom of 2002–11 – enjoying standards of living that have turned out to be unsustainable. Our failure now to deal with the problems that have accumulated since the turn of the century will compound the problems that Australians will have to deal with at some later date. A more fundamental contemporary issue of sustainability, the mitigation of climate change, is the subject of Chapter 9.

WHY AND WHERE PRODUCTIVITY IS FALLING

Australia is fortunate to have excellent public institutions with authority, analytic capacity and independent standing that measure, analyse and provide information on productivity and how it changes over time. Between them, the Australian Bureau of Statistics and the Productivity Commission publish information for policymaking that is superior to that available in almost any other country.

I will use the terms 'total productivity' or simply 'productivity' to avoid repeating the mouthfuls of 'total factor productivity' or 'multi-factor productivity'. I will also use the term 'labour productivity' to mean the value of economic output for each unit of labour input.

For most of our history from Federation, Australia's total productivity growth was unimpressive by the standards of developed countries. That is why we gradually slid down the world league tables for average standards of living, from the top to the lower middle, through the first eight decades of the twentieth century.

That all changed in the Reform Era, and for a while in the 1990s we enjoyed the highest productivity growth of all developed countries, as discussed in Chapter 5. Productivity growth then slowed down sharply. There was no growth at all from 2003 – an early year in the Great Australian Complacency and the beginning of the China resources boom. From 2006 until 2010–11, the latest year for which we have data, total productivity fell.

The narrower measure of labour productivity behaved differently. Labour productivity growth also fell from early in the twenty-first century, but not by as much. And it has picked up recently, returning to high levels in 2012.

Total productivity is the better measure of contributions to higher living standards. Labour productivity can rise either because capital and labour resources are being used more efficiently, or because the amount of capital provided to each worker increases. Capital has a cost, and it is not certain that rising labour productivity from the use of more capital increases living standards. But an increase in the efficiency with which both capital and labour are used – total productivity – unequivocally leads to higher incomes and living standards.

The Bureau of Statistics and the Productivity Commission have recently shown that the decline in total productivity from 2007 to 2012 was concentrated overwhelmingly in four big sectors: mining, utilities (mainly electricity and water), manufacturing and financial services. In the last year for which we have data, 2011–12, productivity had turned around and was growing again in manufacturing, but was sliding even more rapidly in the three other areas.

The declines in productivity in mining and utilities are shocking. Productivity fell at an average rate of 8.4 per cent per annum in mining and 4.5 per cent in utilities from 2007–08 to 2011–12, and by 10.5 per cent and 5.4

per cent respectively in 2011–12. Outside these industries, productivity was merely stagnant.

The causes of falling productivity are different in each of the four sectors. For mining, it was an immediate consequence of the resources boom. High resources investment adds to the capital stock immediately but to production volumes only over a number of years. This shows up at first as declining productivity, and is partially corrected later as capital expenditure falls and exports increase.

Much investment in the boom has been highly productive and has increased the value of the companies that have undertaken it. Some has been wasteful and has been written down with the retreat of the boom through 2012 and 2013. The productive and the wasteful investment alike reduce productivity in the short term. This picture changes when operations commence from the productive new capacity. The wasteful investment continues to weigh down productivity (although not productivity growth) until its depreciation many years after the initial expenditure.

Productivity in mining has also been reduced because management pays less attention to containing costs when prices are high and margins prodigious. The good reason for doing this is that when profits are extremely high, it makes sense for management to put more effort into increasing production; the bad reason is the human tendency to apply less rigour to reducing costs when things seem to be going well. Difficult tasks that do not need to be done are less likely to be done. This 'less attention' source of declining productivity is corrected when falling commodity prices cause managers to shift their focus to cutting costs. This has been occurring with speed and intensity through 2013.

Finally, the large expansion of mining production in the third phase of the resources boom involves bringing lower-quality mineral deposits into production. This also reduces productivity.

The resources industries are highly competitive and operating within an international environment. The spectacular decline in productivity through the boom will turn around in the period ahead (without productivity returning to its old levels) and does not represent a serious problem for the Australian economy.

By contrast, the decline in productivity in the utilities and especially in electricity *is* a problem. It is a recent phenomenon, dating from early this century, with the biggest deterioration occurring since the introduction of new regulatory arrangements in 2006. There has been more than $100 billion of capital expenditure on the utilities over the past four years. (This investment is several times the expected cost of the National Broadband Network in the whole period from commencement in 2010 to expected completion in 2021.) Yet while new investment has been immense, output from the utilities has declined.

It is argued that large investments have been necessary in recent years to improve the reliability of supply, including by remedying underinvestment in the networks in earlier years. There is a little in that argument – which then suggests that part of the gain in productivity that the Bureau of Statistics, Productivity Commission and I have claimed for the first decade of privatisation and corporatisation in the 1990s was illusory.

For electricity, it is argued as well that the regulation of carbon emissions and the expansion of renewable energy have reduced productivity. That is a small part of the story. The proliferation of small programmes to reduce emissions from about 2005 had some negative effect. The replacement of the smaller schemes by carbon pricing and the broadly based Renewable Energy Target will allow emission reductions with smaller losses.

A bigger story is that the authorities have imposed reliability standards – for example, on the expected frequency of electricity blackouts – that bear no close relationship to economic value or community preferences. But the factor accounting for most of the wasteful investment in electricity is flawed regulatory arrangements. The flaws could be readily and rapidly corrected, although not without political difficulties.

What about water? Here, the marked reduction in winter rainfall and run-off into dams in southwestern Australia at least is recognised by climate scientists as an early footprint of human-induced climate change. Changes in patterns of rainfall and run-off have affected the old water-supply systems for all of the large

Australian cities. Questions can be asked about whether the two desalination plants installed in Perth and one each in Adelaide, Melbourne, Sydney and Brisbane were the most cost-effective responses to the decline in old patterns of river and stream flow into the dams. Whatever the answer to that question, any response to the changing climate that provided reliable water supply to large cities was going to involve large costs just to match the output levels of the years when rain-fed dams did the job. Now that the desalination plants have been built, they will provide the necessary supplementary water-supply capacity for a number of years and cease to be a drag on productivity growth.

Financial services and insurance is the largest sector covered by the Australian Bureau of Statistics' measurement of productivity. There are significant barriers to entry in these industries, some of regulatory origin. Competition has declined in the aftermath of the Great Crash of 2008. As in mining, high profit margins have reduced the pressure to cut costs.

There are opportunities for improvement over time through increased competition. The sector should be attractive for new players, with higher profit margins and rates of return on capital than anywhere else in the developed world.

For manufacturing, the decline in productivity is partly a consequence of the resources boom. The high real exchange rate has been reducing domestic and international sales, and these declining sales are spread over a fixed capital base. From the second quarter of 2013, the improvement of Australian competitiveness through the depreciation of the Australian dollar can be expected to expand sales.

Most of the manufacturing sector is operating in a highly competitive global market, in which there are powerful incentives to absorb efficient practices. Corners of the sector, however, remain or hope to become protected by higher tariffs, anti-dumping and local procurement arrangements, subsidies from commonwealth or state budgets, or idiosyncratic local standards. The aftermath of a large real depreciation in the exchange rate would provide a congenial economic as well as political environment for the swift removal of all remaining barriers to free international trade.

So the four sectors that have contributed most to the productivity decline of the early twenty-first century are in the process of considerable if incomplete correction (mining); would be set upon a path to correction with a large real depreciation of the Australian dollar and the removal of remaining protection (manufacturing); would see a radical improvement in productivity through reforms that are technically straightforward but politically challenging (utilities); or will face large productivity problems for which increased competition would seem to be a necessary part of any solution (financial services).

HOW TO RAISE PRODUCTIVITY

Recent studies have identified many opportunities to increase productivity across the Australian economy. There are a few opportunities for transformational gains, but for the most part we are looking at large numbers of modest incremental gains. The latter can add up to large and eventually transformational improvements, but that will take many years of effective effort.

Each step in productivity-raising reform is politically difficult in isolation, with the gains from each seeming too small to warrant the political effort and cost. Success is much more likely if many productivity-enhancing changes are presented together as a large programme of reform. Vociferous critics of single steps will have difficulty in arguing public-interest reasons for opposing the programme as a whole. Many of the opportunities for improvement will also require reform of our federal system (as discussed in Chapter 7).

It is valuable to distinguish between measures that will have their main effect over the next few years, in the aftermath of the China resources boom, and those that are more long-term. The Immediate List comprises measures that could reduce prices in the early years. The Long-Term List comprises reforms that require time for preparation and implementation, and for their effects to flow through to prices.

MONOPOLIES AND FLAWED REGULATIONS

Productivity-raising reform in one industry can reduce costs to consumers and other industries. Every percentage point by which consumer prices are reduced by this means is one percentage point less that living standards have to decline. Do enough of it, and we may be able to maintain full employment after the boom without much of a decline in living standards at all.

At the top of the Immediate List are measures to increase competition in trade and reduce unnecessarily high profit margins resulting from monopoly power. The potential gains from increased competition are large. There are many examples of the same goods being sold at much higher prices in Australia than in other developed countries, with the discrepancy growing wider through the boom.

A longstanding Australian problem was exacerbated when margins increased as our dollar appreciated against other currencies without the saving being fully passed through to consumers. The margins for many imported goods and services became so large through the Great Complacency that they encouraged new entrants into the retail trade to use the internet rather than the old sales platforms.

More generally, inflated profit margins create opportunities for newcomers whose presence could transform the competitive environment. There are opportunities in retail trade, retail sales of electricity and gas, and banking. The regulatory authorities can assist by removing constraints on competitive behaviour and facilitating entry. The government, with the Australian Competition and Consumer Commission, took steps to remove covenants from shopping mall leases that restricted competition among supermarkets until 2009; the effects of this change will grow over time, and need to be protected and nurtured.

A second set of issues high on the Immediate List involves the reform of pricing arrangements for the natural local monopolies – the utilities (electricity first of all), tollways and civil aviation facilities. Such reform would alter expectations of profits from established businesses and therefore asset values. Legal constraints vary from case to case, but comprehensive economy-wide reform will need deft management to negotiate wider boundaries of change within the law.

Electricity provides an example of both the opportunity and the challenge. The owners of the poles and wires, which represent considerably more than half of the retail cost of electricity, receive a guaranteed rate of return that is extremely high for investment that has little more risk than a government bond. Consumers are slugged twice. They pay an unnecessarily high rate of return on past investments. And then the high rate of return for low-risk investment encourages wasteful overinvestment, on which the consumer must pay the guaranteed return. If the high rates of return on past investments were promptly reduced to economically rational levels, there would be a once-and-for-all reduction in electricity prices. This could be done without a disruption of established arrangements as five-year pricing arrangements come up for renewal. The regulators have been working on other measures to reduce the amount of capital invested in future expansion of the network. 'Time-of-day' pricing, for example, can shift demand from peak to other periods, which allows more power to be carried without investing to increase the capacity of the network.

The problem of overinvestment has been greater for the state-owned than the privately owned electricity networks. However, privatisation alone will not solve the problem of distorted price regulation. The privatisation of such assets should come after the economically rational reform of price regulation. There is a basis for the current Queensland premier's caution about rushing to privatisation of what he has described as natural monopolies.

Reform of pricing for utilities and other local monopolies is urgent as we seek to achieve real depreciation. Higher electricity prices and lower growth in incomes may cause falls in electricity demand. Under current regulatory arrangements with high guaranteed rates of return, prices rise in proportion to any such fall – leading to another round of higher prices and reduced demand.

Gas is a special problem for real depreciation. Eastern Australia (from Queensland to South Australia) has had low gas prices by international standards since the Bass Strait fields were opened in the late 1960s – much lower than the United States. Both eastern Australia and the United States have experienced large increases in gas reserves as a result of the introduction of new technologies in recent years – Australia's proportionately much bigger than those of the United States.

The United States effectively banned liquefaction of gas for export, and the increase in reserves led to big falls in price. From this year it is cautiously licensing export projects, taking care to avoid pushing up prices too much. By contrast, Australia has allowed the free export of gas, and the development of export facilities is a major part of the contemporary resources boom and from now on a majority of its investment phase. As exports come on-stream, domestic gas prices will rise to export parity (East Asian prices, less liquefaction and transport costs). This would have happened even if coal-seam gas developments had proceeded as rapidly as once anticipated; the slowing of development in response to local resistance has meant that temporary shortages of supply may push gas prices even higher. Even without these temporary shortages, eastern Australian gas prices are in the process of shifting from being much lower than those of the United States to being two or three times higher.

The proportionate increase in gas prices will be large. This will raise the cost of living at the same time as import prices are rising from currency depreciation. It is an unwelcome additional pressure at a difficult time of adjustment to the end of the boom.

Does this add up to a reason for intervention in free export policies? Some Australian business interests think so and have advocated going part of the way towards the US position of export restriction with a domestic reservation policy. If we were heading down that route, it would be economically more efficient to spread the costs of 'reservation' over established as well as new capacity, by taxing exports and using the proceeds to reduce the price of domestic sales. I do not favour this approach, as the long-term national economic cost would be high. However, it must be recognised that large increases in gas prices strengthen the headwinds facing the nation.

Many tollway fees and some other transport prices under public–private partnerships are set by allowing a margin above the increase in the consumer price index. This is a problem with currency depreciation, which will push up the consumer price index. Without pricing reform, this will make it harder to turn a fall in the dollar into a real depreciation. A number of private investments in tollways are under financial stress as demand falls below earlier expectations, and their owners are seeking changes in the negotiated arrangements. This may create an opportunity to renegotiate unsatisfactory pricing agreements.

BARRIERS TO INTERNATIONAL TRADE

A third item on the Immediate List is the removal of unnecessary costs from international transactions.

Australia's isolation from the main centres of the world economy is an obstacle to our reaching the highest levels of productivity. Unnecessary trade barriers paired with unnecessarily high international transport and communications costs increase the 'economic distance' between Australia and other countries.

The depreciation of the dollar would provide a congenial context for removing what remains of Australian protection against imports. All protected industries would gain far more from the anticipated fall in the dollar than they would lose from the ending of protection. The removal would extend to all tariffs, anti-dumping and local procurement arrangements, and unusual domestic standards that have no justification in a genuine concern for safety or other public policy objectives. This would allow Australia to participate in the fine intra-industry specialisation that has become the main element of Asian trade expansion over the last decade, and make it clear to the managers of businesses operating in Australia that their future lies in improved competitiveness and deep engagement with the international economy. If the removal were implemented at the same time as subsidies to trade-exposed industries were removed, the savings from subsidies would pay for the reductions in import duties, with a substantial margin left over to go towards other things.

While preferential trade agreements are generally of low and sometimes of negative value, there are strong reasons now to bring negotiations with China to a positive conclusion. China has made agreements with New Zealand and those countries in the Association of Southeast Asian Nations that allow their suppliers superior access to Chinese agricultural markets in competition with Australian suppliers. A preferential trade agreement of our own is the only practical early way to remove discrimination against our agricultural exports.

The Chinese government has made the matching of US treatment by the Foreign Investment Review Board a condition of entering a preferential trade agreement with Australia. Restrictions on foreign investment in general and Chinese investment in particular have support in parts of our polity. They also have costs – rather more now in relation to Chinese investment than ever in relation to American. I can see no economic benefit from the current review process. Security issues may arise in relation to particular investments. These are best handled by specialist agencies, case by case on their merits.

THE URGENT NEED FOR TAX REFORM

Rather than set out a comprehensive reform agenda, I simply note here for the Long-Term List three prominent issues – taxation, competition and industrial relations – that illustrate the nature of the opportunity and the challenge that must be met. It is common for people to think of tax reform as a reduction in the amount of tax they pay. For this reason, reform is always hard when there is no large overall cut on offer. The tax reform of 2000 was rendered politically more palatable because it reduced the overall tax burden by 1 per cent of GDP. But there is no room for overall tax reduction in the Dog Days.

Personal income tax collections have been rising in real terms and as a proportion of the economy since the tax cuts that followed the 2007 election. The status quo delivers a steady increase in receipts as inflation moves taxpayers into higher tax brackets. But receipts from all other large sources have been declining as a share of national income.

The proportion of national income collected by the GST has been falling. Since 2011–12, the proportion collected as corporate income tax has also been falling with the huge growth in deductions from the resources investment boom, and will continue to do so for several years. A large amount of revenue is currently collected from the sale of carbon emissions permits, but this is set to fall, at least for a while, with the linking of the Australian to the European carbon price from 2014 or 2015.

The proportion of national income collected as excise has been falling since the indexation of fuel tax was abolished in 2001, and will continue to do so until indexation is restored. The increase in tobacco excise in 2013 only temporarily stalled this decline.

Capital-gains tax receipts as a proportion of the economy have fallen with the halving of tax rates in 2000 and declining rates of asset appreciation since the Great Crash of 2008. With cuts in the capital-gains tax, there were new opportunities to avoid paying personal income tax through the conversion of income into capital gains.

The extraordinary superannuation taxation changes of 2006 effectively exempted large numbers of prosperous older Australians from income tax obligations. Until a generation ago, both state and federal governments collected large amounts of money from estate and gift duties – as the governments of the United States, the United Kingdom and most other developed countries still do. These taxes now yield nothing in Australia.

At the state level, the proportion of national income collected as stamp duties has fallen with the easing of the early 21st-century housing boom. The payroll tax was once a major source of state revenue; it has been whittled away by successive exemptions and reductions.

That more and more of the load is carried by income tax payers with limited opportunities for avoiding taxation is economically distorting, unfair and probably politically unsustainable.

There is no sign in the electorate of any Australian preference for reducing public expenditure as a share of the economy. The Australian Treasury's periodic Inter-Generational Reports tell us that the ageing population alone, without any improvement of services, is driving us towards an increase of 4.7 per cent of GDP in demand for public services and income support by mid-century.

And we enter 2014 with an expected deficit in the commonwealth budget over 1 per cent of GDP and the likelihood that the combined state deficits will be very large (if they are measured in the same way as commonwealth deficits).

The Australian business taxation system imposes unnecessarily high economic costs and there would be productivity gains from fundamental reform. The field of tax reform is full of the casualties of past wars over policy. We will not get a good outcome from a new attempt unless we each stop picking at the scars from old battles. We are most likely to succeed if we go back to first principles and ask how Australia can best raise an adequate amount of revenue at low economic cost, resulting in a distribution of the tax burden that is economically efficient and fair.

That means recognising the merits of applying similar tax rates to all income – whether it accrues as cash payments for work, or as dividends, or capital gains, or fringe benefits. It means looking again at the special treatment of superannuation. It means being prepared to assess, with an open mind, the contribution that carbon pricing can make to public revenues. It means being prepared to consider extending, and increasing the rate of, the GST.

Answering the question of how Australia can meet its revenue requirements at lowest costs involves being open to fundamental change in the structure of corporate taxation, so as to minimise the cost of capital to industries in which competition and open entry to all opportunities mean that there are no durable rents. It means being open to the efficient taxation of economic rent – returns above the minimum necessary to attract capital to an activity – including generally applicable rent taxes across all of the resource industries, and on oligopolistic rents elsewhere in the economy.

The new government has said that it will establish a taxation review. This is the place to examine our revenue system from first principles. It has also said that it will establish a review of federal financial relations. The two reviews are closely related to each other and should be undertaken in parallel. The tax review needs to be expert, like the Henry Review, and independent, unlike the Henry Review. Part of its role should be to synthesise, assess and extend the results of past work. Close analysis from a public interest perspective would reveal that the proposal most favoured by business at present – a simple cut in company income tax rates without structural reform – would not be a cost-effective approach to tax reform. This time the resulting report should be made available for extensive public discussion before the government makes policy decisions.

THE WORK OF BREAKING UP MONOPOLIES IS NEVER DONE

A second major item for the Long-Term List is the promotion of competition, along with the efficient regulation of prices and quality standards. This is one area where some progress has been made over the past half a dozen years, including by the Australian Competition and Consumer Commission.

The task of maintaining a competitive economy is never done. Adam Smith advised us at the beginnings of the modern economy that 'people of the same trade seldom meet together, even for merriment and diversion, but the conversation ends in a conspiracy against the public, or in some contrivance to raise prices'.

The removal of exchange controls and most protection in the Reform Era introduced a high degree of competition into the one-third of the Australian economy directly exposed to international trade. Competition policy in the late 1980s and 1990s made markets more contestable in much of the rest of the economy. However, reform was incomplete, and there was backsliding during the Great Complacency.

One upshot of the trend to privatisation and corporatisation was the creation of utilities and suppliers of transport services, and of investors in public–private partnerships and private contractors to government, which were in positions to exercise monopolistic or oligopolistic power. Problems in these parts of the economy not exposed to international competition contributed substantially to the early 21st-century decline in productivity. There are opportunities here for large gains, although the agenda is complex and subtle. Some reforms must await long periods of analysis, consultation and negotiation, and development of new administrative structures.

In the third area of reform for the Long-Term List, industrial relations, it is relevant that we have seen frequent change for over two decades now. As Prime Minister Tony Abbott says, it is important that the pendulum cease its oscillation. Stability will bring large economic and social benefits.

The chances of maintaining full employment following the end of the China resources boom would be higher if statutory minimum wages were held steady in response to higher import prices. But this will be difficult in our democratic polity without reform of taxation and social security payments to help maintain household incomes while also increasing incentives to participate in the labour market (as discussed in the next chapter). For the rest, it is important that formal arrangements do not stand in the way of management and employees working out more productive means of doing things and sharing the benefits.

CHAPTER 7
POPULATION, PARTICIPATION AND EQUITY

A reform programme must be widely seen to be fair if it is to have any chance of enduring success in our democratic polity. The economic underperformance that would be the future companion of a 'business as usual' approach tends naturally to generate unfair outcomes. It concentrates the burden of reduced living standards on the unemployed, on those who are discouraged from work, on those whose skills lose value because they are unable to use them, and on owners of small businesses which are forced to close.

Full employment with high participation, adequate income support for disadvantaged Australians, universal access to good basic health and education, and an effective progressive tax system are the most important contributors to equity in Australia. The recent election campaign confirmed that there is common ground across the polity on the need for a more effective provision for the advancement of Indigenous Australians and a more substantial provision for that of Australians with disabilities.

The big challenge in the period ahead is a conservative one: to maintain these elements of an equitable society through tough times. A number of things will make this difficult: pressure on the budget and incomes through the adjustment to the end of the resources boom; the increased cost of an ageing population; the corrosion of the tax base through piecemeal reduction and abolition of taxes, especially over recent times of high prosperity; and the political barriers facing reform to raise efficiency in the delivery of government services at the mature end of the Great Complacency.

The challenge is to raise adequate revenue to fund the state and its education, health and social security programmes without unnecessarily reducing investment and economic growth. More generally, an economically successful society – with rising productivity, average incomes and taxable capacity – is more likely to be able to provide adequately for public services and transfer payments. The productivity agenda discussed in the previous chapter is therefore important to equity.

This chapter discusses a few other issues important to equity – issues related to population, participation and employment. I begin with a discussion of immigration and population, because it is sometimes thought that pulling back on them in hard times will help Australians who are already here. These issues are bound to arise again when jobs become more difficult to find as the resources boom recedes.

IMMIGRATION HELPS POORER AUSTRALIANS

Since World War II, high immigration has kept the Australian population growing much more rapidly than in other developed countries. As a result, our population has also aged much more slowly than that of comparable nations. This has been a source of continuing economic dynamism.

Will this continue in the Dog Days? If the economy slows and jobs are fewer, population growth will automatically ease back. Migrants from New Zealand, and family reunion and business migrants, will come in fewer numbers. Other immigration categories are capped, and the caps tend to be wound back at times of economic downturn and high unemployment. The combination of these two influences caused immigration and population growth to fall considerably during recent recessions (1974–75, 1982–83 and 1990–91) and their aftermaths.

Does lower immigration and population growth make it easier to restore full employment during and after a downturn? The evidence mainly says 'no'. It may even exacerbate unemployment. Immigration contributes as much to *demand* for labour and employment as it does to *supply*. Confidence in steady population growth underpins investment in housing and infrastructure. During downturns, population growth reduces the chances of Australia sharing with other developed countries the large falls in house prices that cause new residential construction to stop. Immigration makes it easier to attract international capital, which is required to employ an expanding workforce productively.

The tendency for Australian governments in modern times to fund major capital expenditure out of current revenue has contributed to underinvestment in infrastructure, which has led to immigration being associated with a deterioration in transport and other urban services. Catching up with a backlog of investment in such infrastructure would make a positive contribution to the economy as the resources boom recedes. This opportunity would not be so readily available in an economy without population growth.

So it is unlikely that cuts to immigration would help to reduce unemployment in the period ahead. But what about the longer-term effects? Here, too, a sustained cut in skilled and educated immigration will in fact eventually *lower* the average incomes of Australians, especially those with less economically valuable skills and on lower incomes.

This is an 'on balance' judgment, as there are negative as well as positive effects. Negatively, the spreading of a finite endowment of valuable natural resources among a larger number of people reduces the amount of natural resource rent that is available to each Australian.

Positively, there are economies of scale in supply of many national services and public goods. These economies are crucially important for Australia's civic and cultural assets (literature, theatre, sporting competitions, media, economic debate, universities, foreign relations and defence). In a country with a widely dispersed population of modest size, there are also economies of scale in national transport and communications infrastructure. A larger and more concentrated population allows more competition among the suppliers of goods and services who are not kept on their toes by products from abroad. What matters for civic and cultural assets and infrastructure are average rates of population growth over long periods rather than whether high rates of immigration are maintained through recession.

Also positively, immigration affects the composition of the population in two ways that are important for national economic performance: age and skill structures. All developed countries have fertility below replacement levels and declining proportions of working-age people. This means that output per worker must rise over time to keep output and incomes per person steady. However, immigration tends to increase the proportion of working-age people in the population, especially since Australian policy gives priority to the relatively young.

Immigration also affects the average level of skills in the community. There are remarkable differences between Australian and US approaches to immigration. The United States in practice (taking into account large-scale illegal arrivals) favours unskilled immigration, so that newcomers compete with and lower the employment opportunities and wages of poorer Americans. We do the opposite, more powerfully since the mid-1990s, so that immigration increases the employment prospects and wages of poorer Australians. This is one reason why income disparities have widened much more in the United States than in Australia over the past generation.

Not all categories of immigration have the same mix of skills and education. Refugees and family immigrants tend to be less educated; skilled (including '457-visa' temporary workers) and business migrants tend to be more so. The skilled categories often bear the brunt of discretionary cutbacks during recessions.

The 457-visa question was prominent in Australian politics in the first half of 2013 and is bound to become important again as unemployment rises. The skilled nature of 457-visa migrants helps maintain the living standards of relatively unskilled Australians. But the 'temporary' nature of these migrants is problematic if this becomes the normal way of supplying skills, rather than a response to specific shortages.

AUSTRALIAN IMMIGRATION DOESN'T DAMAGE GLOBAL SUSTAINABILITY

Since the 1970s, some Australians have opposed high immigration on sustainability grounds. To the extent that the concern is about the Australian environment, it has a place in a debate about conservation. My own view is that intelligent (and economically rational) planning of cities and sound conservation policy can reconcile a larger Australian population with environmental amenity.

To the extent that the concern is about a global environmental problem, it is largely misplaced. Yes, there is a global population problem – increasingly concentrated in Africa and other regions in which economic development was late to start and has yet to bear rich fruits. Fertility rates remain well above replacement levels in most countries with low living standards. While antinatal policies have been effective in China and Singapore, these do not seem to be acceptable or replicable outside East Asia. Economic development is the only known instrument that reliably reduces fertility, although the provision of information and technology to women in developing countries can help.

To the extent that migration to Australia has any effect on global population, it helps to slow the increase – fertility declines on average among people who migrate here from poorer countries.

An argument has been made in recent years that immigration should be reduced because it makes it more difficult for Australia to contribute its fair share in the fight against climate change by meeting targets for reducing greenhouse gas emissions. A more challenging version of this view notes that Australian emissions per person are well above those in many of the countries from which our migrants come. But if the world is to avoid dangerous climate change, average emissions in Australia and in other countries will have to converge on some low figure. The world will be thinking of emissions entitlements per person, and Australia's entitlements will be larger if immigrants increase our population. The international effort will not be helped or hindered by the location of a bit less of the globe's emissions in the country of origin and a bit more in Australia.

WHAT WE MEAN BY PARTICIPATION AND EMPLOYMENT TODAY

However many Australians there are, average incomes are mainly determined by productivity, participation (the hours that people want to work compared with the hours available) and how close we are to full employment (the hours worked compared with the hours people want to work). If average incomes fall because of higher unemployment, it is likely that a high proportion of the loss will accrue to Australians with relatively low incomes and wealth.

Australians' ideas about how much they want to work under varying circumstances and at different times in their lives have changed radically over the past one to two generations. What the Adelaide economist Sue Richardson calls the 'Harvester Judgment family' of a man who works full-time for pay, a woman who works at home without pay, and two or three dependent children, once ubiquitous, is now a small minority.

Standard unemployment data simply compare the number of people who are employed (those who have worked for an hour in the last week) with the number who are unemployed (those who were looking for work in the past week but did not work for an hour). The Australian Bureau of Statistics and some private pollsters now provide estimates of people who are not looking for work but would like to work. These new measures still do not take into account gaps between hours worked and the hours people would like to work.

However you measure it, the labour market was strong in 2011 and has steadily weakened since then. The single factor that I think gets closest to measuring the state of the labour market is monthly hours worked per person over fifteen years. This ratio has been falling since late 2011 (see Chart 1). It is not falling as rapidly as during the 1990–91 recession, but it is still heading consistently lower more than two years into the downturn, when employment was already heading up at the same distance from the peak in the early 1990s.

The immediate task is to have the economy generate more jobs relative to the adult population – to stabilise the employment ratios and then turn them around. Then the task is to increase the participation of all sorts of Australians if they want to work for pay – old people, mothers with children of various ages or who have ceased to have dependent children, people on disability benefits, people with disabilities who are not on benefits, Indigenous Australians in remote communities and others.

We used to think and write and talk a lot about how to increase employment back in the 1990s, because unemployment was high. The issue went away during the second half of the long boom – hours worked per adult remained reasonably strong here even in the year after the Great Crash, when they shrunk disastrously in most of the developed world. But we are moving towards the lowest monthly hours worked and highest unemployment of the twenty-first century. It will be time for us to go back to the ideas about how to increase employment that we were considering in the '90s.

The most important thing that we can do is to make sure we sustainably increase demand in the economy. But that is still likely to leave a lot of relatively unskilled people wanting more hours of work than are available to them.

Minimum wages for unskilled workers, high by international standards in the 1990s, are further out of line with other countries now. At the exchange rates of early 2013, they were twice what minimum wages are in the United States, and one and a half times those of European countries with similar systems. While high minimum wages raise the incomes of low-income working households in which there is no unemployment, at Australian (as distinct from US) levels they discourage employment of unskilled people. This has not been a large problem through the boom, but it will be more and more important in the harder times ahead, because high minimum wages inhibit growth in jobs for workers on the edge of the labour force.

In 1998, the 'Five Economists', coordinated by the then director of the Melbourne Institute at the University of Melbourne, Peter Dawkins, put forward a proposal to encourage increases in employment while maintaining the incomes of families with members earning the minimum wage, and to reconcile higher social security payments with stronger incentives for workforce participation. This proposal was built around the provision of an earned income tax credit alongside a freeze in minimum wages.

The Five Economists' proposal was a response to two features of the economy at that time: persistent high unemployment among low-skilled workers; and high effective tax rates on the extra income received by workers when income tax and the withdrawal of social security payments were taken into account.

We have entered another period of unsatisfactory jobs growth, and the problem is again most severe for low-skilled workers. It is time to consider once more proposals like those of the Five Economists.

WAYS TO MARRY WELFARE AND EMPLOYMENT

Australia's social security system succeeds in looking after low-income people reasonably well by international and historical standards, at a relatively low cost (measured as a share of GDP). Total welfare spending will increase under current policies as we go through the tough period for employment after the resources boom. An increased targeting of social security payments would be a fair way of constraining payments within limits that are consistent with fiscal sustainability. But tighter tapers increase the marginal effective tax rates that affect choices about how much paid work to do. It is important to find ways to improve the trade-off between social security and the incentive to work.

While the Five Economists suggested an earned income tax credit, the commonwealth introduced some years ago an instrument with similar features, the Low Income Tax Offset (LITO). One or other could serve in contemporary circumstances; the choice would be based on contemporary analysis.

An increase in the LITO would raise the after-tax incomes of low-wage workers without increasing labour costs to employers and with a minimal increase in the disincentive to work for low-skilled workers. That would ease the reality and to some extent the perception that it is unfair to freeze unskilled workers' incomes under the new circumstances.

Meanwhile, it would fit with the larger reform programme, and with the prime minister's approach to policymaking, for the government to establish a review of social security in parallel with the review of taxation. This would build on the work of the Howard government's McClure Review. It would examine more far-reaching changes to assist low-income households while increasing incentives for all potential workers. It would take a look at the relationship of social security and labour force participation in new circumstances: an older population that is, on the whole, healthier; and a much higher proportion of the population on disability benefits.

This comprehensive review would look at various forms of 'negative income tax'. Such a system aims to reconcile substantial payments to low-income households with the incentive to enter the workforce. It would initially be focused on the labour force – full-time and part-time workers as well as the unemployed.

The new arrangements in the first instance would cover everyone who demonstrated that they were in the labour force. A basic payment would be made at the rate corresponding to the Newstart unemployment allowance and paid fortnightly into the recipient's bank account. All income would be taxed from the first dollar.

A plan would be developed gradually to extend coverage. People with disabilities would receive higher rates of basic payment, as would those above a specified age (with the qualifying age for the additional payments increasing over time to recognise longer life and better health beyond the old 'retirement age'). Primary carers with children below a specified age would qualify for a substantial basic payment, whether or not they were currently members of the labour force, thereby reducing disincentives to paid work.

The new arrangements would replace the tax-free threshold, the lowest tranches of the current income tax, the LITO, Newstart and eventually as wide a range of transfer payments as possible. Every dollar earned would be taxed at the same basic rate, up to some point above average earnings. Tax rates and thresholds on higher incomes would not be changed. The basic payment would be withdrawn as asset thresholds were crossed. Unlike overlapping income tests, this would not act as a disincentive to paid work.

In his book *Battlelines*, the prime minister notes that when he was a minister in the Howard government, a public service taskforce considered the comprehensive change needed to produce a system along these lines. He clearly saw advantages to this approach, but with a basic tax rate of 40 per cent it was judged to be too expensive. I suspect that the proposal considered by the taskforce might have started with wider coverage than I am suggesting here. In any case, the costs would be lower now, following successive income tax cuts, the raising of the tax-free threshold to $18,200, the introduction and possible extension of the LITO, and various elongations of the tapers for withdrawal of social security payments.

Such a reform of the social security system would have net budgetary costs, but these would not go up in smoke. To the extent that the reform achieved its purpose of increasing participation in the workforce, it would contribute to the budget as well as to economic output. Higher participation could be expected to extend over many parts of the population: the young, the old, the disabled and, above all, carers of children who are second earners in a household. As such, it would improve the prospects for maintaining equity in the process of adjustment to the end of the boom, and for maintaining community support for a far-reaching reform programme.

CHAPTER 8
THE PUBLIC SECTOR AND THE FEDERATION

Under Australia's federal system of government, most major services are delivered by the states, but the overwhelming proportion of revenue is collected by the commonwealth. The mismatch of funding and responsibilities is now a major barrier to effective government. Reform in this arcane, complex and politically fraught field is essential to making the most of Australia's long-term opportunities.

Economists call the gap between revenue and responsibilities 'vertical fiscal imbalance'. Australia's extreme imbalance has emerged over more than a century of practice by commonwealth and state governments, as well as constitutional interpretation by the High Court of Australia. The states once administered a number of taxes that are now only applied by the commonwealth (income tax; retail sales taxes on fuels, tobacco products and alcoholic beverages) or not at all (inheritance and gift duties). Furthermore, the recent (2013) High Court judgment in *Fortescue v. the Commonwealth* has confirmed the constitutional validity of the commonwealth's recent entry into another field once exclusively occupied by the states: taxation of resource rents for on-shore projects.

From 1971, the commonwealth agreed that the states would have exclusive power to levy the payroll tax with its considerable revenue-raising potential. Over the past three decades the states have whittled its revenue-raising power away bit by bit with exemptions and reductions. Ironically, this was encouraged by business lobbies, which were at the same time seeking increases in the GST, which has much the same effect. The business pressure to reduce the payroll tax and increase the value-added tax reflected a confusion over the point of collection of a tax and the people upon whom its burden ultimately falls.

Not only did the states corrode much of their existing tax base, but they rejected an offer by the Fraser government in the late 1970s to share the proceeds of the income tax. They can be seen as joint authors of their own impecuniousness. Be that as it may, their continuing financial problems affect all Australians.

The gap in funding for state-supplied services is filled by commonwealth grants of two kinds: general purpose and specific. The latter are made available on the condition that the states spend them in ways approved by the commonwealth. Both forms of grants are problematic, albeit for different reasons.

General purpose grants comprise the revenue collected by the commonwealth from the GST. The smaller states succeeded in having this distributed according to the unique Australian system of 'horizontal fiscal equalisation', which is administered by the Commonwealth Grants Commission. At the time that the GST was introduced, the two largest states, New South Wales and Victoria, received less than their population share of the grants that the proceeds of the tax were meant to replace, while all the other states and territories were recipients of more than their share. The Victorian government saw merit in the GST as an innovation in public policy and, in an act of national leadership, put aside its state interest to agree to the allocation of funds through horizontal fiscal equalisation. The NSW government was left alone to resist the new system and was unsuccessful. The inadvertent effect of the arrangements for the GST was to expand what had once been a distorting but relatively unimportant element of our fiscal system.

Under the Constitution, the states are responsible for the provision of major services, including health and aged care, the demand for which increases over time as a share of expenditure, while the tax base of the GST is declining. (Health, education and food are excluded from the tax.) And more and more of the goods and services actually covered by the tax are purchased online and so avoid liability.

Special purpose grants are problematic because their spread has meant that virtually all of the states' constitutional responsibilities have become joint responsibilities with the commonwealth. Their pervasive nature removes almost all exclusive initiative from the states and negates much, if not all, of the potential value of the Federation.

The two problems together have ensured an extreme lack of transparency in the national political process. It is practically impossible for the residents of a state to apportion responsibility between the state and federal governments for good or poor performance on critically important matters of economic management and the delivery of services. The consequence is that both state and federal political parties announce commitments that depend for their success on complementary action from the other level of government, and electoral competition focuses on attempts to claim credit for successes and avoid responsibility for failures.

In the first period of the Rudd government, a substantial effort was made to correct these problems with special purpose payments. The organising idea was to orchestrate cooperation between the commonwealth and the states on reducing the number of such payments, by agreeing to broad objectives and monitoring performance against them. Some worthwhile progress was made before the relentless march of business as usual again increased the number of special purpose grants and confirmed the system's dysfunction. This episode demonstrated the need for more fundamental reform.

THE VALUE OF THE FEDERATION

There are widely differing views on the value of a Federation comprising separate states with sovereign powers, compared with the value of a unitary Australian state. My view is that the Federation is potentially of high economic and political and social value to Australia, generating benefits from decentralisation of delivery, from differing public choices on taxation and expenditure, and from opportunities for competition over different ways of delivering services.

But whatever one's views, we are currently in the worst of all possible worlds. The states do not have the fiscal freedom with which to deliver the potential benefits of Federation. And the commonwealth does not have the capacities for effective central exercise of the powers of government.

Reform of federal arrangements might seem a bridge too far. Unfortunately, the problems are so large that without change they will remain a major barrier to the effective delivery of a range of services that are essential to both good economic performance and to equity in Australia, including health, education and transport infrastructure. I put forward for discussion just one set of Long-Term List changes to federal financial relations that would help bring about a higher Australian standard of living.

First, there should be a far-reaching review of commonwealth and state functions, with each being unambiguously allocated to one or other level of government. I would leave constitutional responsibility for funding disability services and Indigenous development unambiguously in the hands of the commonwealth. For the rest, ending ambiguity is more important than how the division of responsibility falls. Whitlam and Abbott once thought that hospitals should lie within the commonwealth's area of responsibility. Rudd suggested during the 2013 election campaign that responsibility for technical and further education should pass to the commonwealth. These would all be matters for discussion.

Second, the imbalance between revenue and responsibility that remains after the reallocation of powers and responsibilities should be met in two ways: the states should make greater use of their power to raise revenue; and all of their revenue from the commonwealth should be unambiguously and irrevocably delivered as general purpose grants.

In the case of tax, there is considerable scope for expanding revenue from a number of relatively efficient sources: payroll, land (on unimproved value rather than transactions) and resource rent taxation.

A review of federal financial relations, which was foreshadowed by the prime minister during the election campaign, will almost certainly leave some imbalance requiring funding from the commonwealth. Specific purpose grants should be avoided. General purpose grants could usefully take all or a specified proportion of some commonwealth taxes. The GST and the MRRT would be candidates.

If any such revenue were entirely transferred to the states, as it is and should continue to be for the GST, the states would take responsibility for decisions on the tax rate and any other changes that affect the amount of revenue collected. Where it is sensible to allow for variation in the rate of a tax among states, each jurisdiction can set the rate within its own boundaries. Where administrative reality requires a common rate of tax across Australia, a constitutional agreement can specify how changes are to be made.

SIMPLIFYING INTERSTATE EQUALISATION

The aim of the Commonwealth Grants Commission's 'horizontal fiscal equalisation' is to give all states and territories the same capacity to provide services to citizens. On the revenue side, a state receives a higher proportion of GST revenue if it collects less revenue per capita than the average when applying the average taxes in the average way. If the 'average' involves an inefficient tax at a high rate, any state or territory that does not apply that tax at that rate will see its share of GST revenue fall. A state with unusually large opportunities for raising revenue from some source (for example, Western Australia for mining royalties) will have its share of GST revenue reduced (after a lag) if it exercises this opportunity.

On the expenditure side, the more it costs to provide services within a state or territory, the higher a proportion of GST revenue this state or territory receives (whether or not it actually provides the services). The extra costs of providing a service are known as 'disabilities'.

The system of horizontal fiscal equalisation diverts the attention of officials whose main responsibility would otherwise be good public policy and administration, especially in the smaller jurisdictions. It obscures and weakens accountability for the consequences of good and poor budget management. It creates financial risks for a state that is reducing the costs of providing services. It systematically penalises states that experience higher rates of economic growth, whether the improved performance comes from luck or good management. And it removes incentives for the application of economically efficient forms and rates of taxation, with this being especially important for the natural resource industries.

An elaborate process of measuring disabilities on raising revenue and provision of services generates a wide range of positive (especially for the Northern Territory, Tasmania and South Australia) and negative (especially for Western Australia, Victoria and New

South Wales) outcomes. One consequence is the emergence of a disproportionately large public sector in the major recipient states.

A new system for the distribution of general purpose grants from the commonwealth obviously requires much discussion and would be contentious. There is no chance of consensus among the states, so leadership must be exercised by the commonwealth. As the source of the revenue being disbursed, it has the authority to take control.

At present, the huge variations in per capita entitlements from the GST revenue pool derive heavily from two sources: the cost of providing services to Indigenous Australians (which are especially important in the Northern Territory) and the greater capacity of Western Australia to generate revenue from mining royalties. There is also a general tendency for the less populous states to receive larger amounts per person (the Northern Territory, Australian Capital Territory, Tasmania and South Australia).

This huge, distorting, opaque and contentious apparatus could be replaced with surprisingly little initial disturbance if there were equal per capita entitlements to the pool of revenue, after making special arrangements for the higher overhead costs of government in smaller states, differences in proportions and locations of Indigenous citizens, and differences in taxable mineral endowments.

The meeting of the minimum costs of government in each jurisdiction can be seen as an unavoidable cost of the Federation. This simple reality could be reflected, in transfers from the common pool, by provision of a lump sum relating to the basic machinery of government. In 2002, Vince Fitzgerald and I suggested a lump sum payment of $100 million to each state and territory. That amount might double if a new system were to be introduced later this decade.

TAXING RESOURCES WITHIN THE FEDERATION

A new approach to mineral rent taxation would be at the core of a new federal compact. Differences in capacity to raise royalties from minerals production are now the major cause of variations across jurisdictions. The Commonwealth Grants Commission distributes this royalty revenue across the states, in proportion to population and with a lag of several years. As a result, the share of Western Australia has declined sharply in recent years and seems likely to continue to do so until the state receives less than half of the average Australian grant per person.

Taxing the resources industry has become a major problem for our Federation. There is a widespread understanding of the need for a fundamental departure from the status quo. This departure cannot be to leave all of the taxation power and revenue with the state of origin: that would be too great a violation of Australian perceptions of interstate equity. And not only Australian: all countries with major inter-regional variations in minerals revenues have mechanisms for substantial redistribution.

One consequence of the averaging away of resource revenues is that the states have little incentive to introduce economically rational levels and forms of taxation and royalties. A consequence of the particular formulae used by the Grants Commission is that the states are fiscally compelled to apply royalties in an economically distorting form.

Simply by way of illustration, let us say that analysis of the public interest identified the optimal form and rate of resource taxation as that of the Petroleum Resource Rent Tax (PRRT), which was legislated for new projects in the mid-1980s. This happens to be close to the form although not the rate of the MRRT introduced in 2011. We can leave aside the transitional arrangements for the MRRT and extension of the PRRT, as these become unimportant in later years.

My suggestion is that the commonwealth should apply the PRRT and MRRT in areas within state jurisdictions at half of what has been the established rate – say 20 per cent. The commonwealth could therefore be seen as utilising half of the 'optimal' taxation capacity of the resources industries. The commonwealth's revenue from this source would be placed in the general purposes grant pool, alongside the GST and some other revenue sources. The states would be invited to occupy the other half of this potential taxation space. Appropriate transitional arrangements would be introduced for established mines – taking account of the fact that investors in the resource industries would be given a number of years' notice of the change.

The commonwealth would invite the state or territory host of a project to apply the MRRT to its half of the taxation capacity. The state could choose to vary the rate from 20 per cent if it wished to do so. The commonwealth would collect the tax for the state. If some states and territories simply chose to duplicate the commonwealth's rate of tax, thus exhausting the taxation capacity, this would be a good outcome for economic efficiency. Alternatively, the state could ask the commonwealth to levy and to collect an additional portion of MRRT or PRRT at a rate of its choosing.

Or else, the state could choose to apply a royalty in a form and at a rate of its choosing. Neither the additional resource rent tax nor the additional royalty would be deductible against the commonwealth resource rent tax, although both would be deductible (not creditable) against commonwealth corporate income tax. So all of the resources revenues would be returned to the states – half directly to the state of origin, and half to the pool for general purpose grants to be allocated across the states and territories.

Good governance and the High Court in *Fortescue v. the Commonwealth* suggest that this result for resource taxation should be achieved through agreement between the commonwealth and the states.

A NEW FEDERAL AGREEMENT

Such an agreement would only be possible in the context of a comprehensive revision of federal financial relations. The political difficulties of this change to the overall structure of federal financial relations would be large, but the suggested arrangements could be phased in over time. This process would be accompanied by guarantees of minimum payments to the states and territories under the new arrangements: for example, the commonwealth could guarantee that a state or territory's share of the general purpose grants pool would not cause the real value of grants (replacing current general purpose and specific purpose payments) to fall by more than 1 per cent per annum. What matters is that we move steadily towards satisfactory long-term arrangements.

The Commonwealth Grants Commission could be given two roles: reporting on the fiscal health of the Federation independently of the political interests of the commonwealth or any state; and assessing the amount of the lump sum payments necessary to cover the minimum overhead costs of government. If one or other state or territory found itself in difficult short-term fiscal circumstances, the independent commission could make recommendations on temporary special grants. This would return the role of the Commonwealth Grants Commission to something like that in the 1930s, when it was first established.

Now, over a century after the federal compact, is a

good time to review thoroughly the distribution of powers between the two levels of sovereign government. This is unlikely to lead to a shrinking of formal commonwealth powers; it may lead to their expansion. But if change in the division of powers is not possible, let us confirm the established division and introduce fiscal arrangements that will allow it to work efficiently. Whatever the outcome of the review, let us establish a norm in which the states have unambiguous fiscal authority within their jurisdictions, and in which the commonwealth's intervention mainly takes the form of provision of advice and comparative information, assessment of performance, analysis of policy and definition of national norms where they are appropriate.

I say mostly, because the dynamics of politics will from time to time propel the commonwealth into areas of state sovereignty. But let us see such initiatives as deviations from a desirable norm.

SOLVING THE TRANSPORT STAND-OFF

In the meantime, we can do something quickly to solve one of the most debilitating problems of the Federation. Nowhere has the cost and absurdity of the overlapping commonwealth and states been greater than in funding major transport infrastructure. Commonwealth and state each undertake to fund part of some major infrastructure project if the other level of government funds the balance

– often after purely political assessments and without consulting one another.

The dysfunction of these arrangements reached bizarre depths when the commonwealth, in early 2013, undertook to fund a proportion of an underground railway across Melbourne if the Victorian government matched its commitment. For its part, the state government undertook to fund a major proportion of an underground *road* across Melbourne if the commonwealth matched *its* commitment. There was no evidence of rigorous analysis of the economic value of the road project – so far as the community was concerned, little evidence of any analysis at all. Whether or not one or other of the projects goes ahead, the electorate will be unable to allocate responsibility for the result.

There is a simple remedy for these problems. The commonwealth would withdraw from decisions on which transport projects should proceed and their implementation. It would establish an independent authority with a strong capacity for analysis. This could be built from Infrastructure Australia. The independent authority would undertake rigorous cost-benefit studies of projects from a national point of view. It would define a list of projects with benefits exceeding costs that would qualify for commonwealth funding. If a state or territory wished to proceed with any project on the list, it could draw down a substantial fixed proportion of the capital expenditure requirements (say, 50 per cent in normal circumstances) as a loan from the commonwealth, at the commonwealth's long-term borrowing rate. The state or territory government would be entirely responsible for the project.

The commonwealth authority would look only at the economic costs and benefits of various projects. It would have no bias for or against particular transport modes: road and rail projects would each be judged according to their economic contribution. The effectiveness of the proposed approach would depend on the quality of analysis and planning within the states. They would need to develop their own independent, transparent assessment mechanisms. In contrast with current practice, state planning would focus on cost-effective integration of the different transport modes.

There is another problem with major infrastructure that is not caused by the federal framework, but which could be eased considerably as part of the proposed reform of federal financing. Australian governments can borrow over long periods at low rates of interest – on average, over the last century, for ten years at around 2 per cent per annum in real terms. It is not obvious that the 'risk' of devoting funds to carefully assessed infrastructure projects is greater than that of spending money in other ways and thereby accepting the risk – indeed, the certainty – of continued increase in transport and congestion costs within our major cities. And yet assessments of public investment in transport infrastructure typically apply discount rates that incorporate allowances for risk that make the rates many times higher than the real cost of borrowing to government.

At the discount rates currently applied to infrastructure projects in Australia, no transformation ever seems worth doing. All major structural change in transport takes many years to implement, and most of the benefits are discounted to trivial values by the use of high discount rates. These are sometimes called market interest rates, although the market rate at which governments can borrow is more like 2 than 7 or 8 per cent in real terms.

For the states, one reason for caution about borrowing for infrastructure is that modest increases in debt may trigger a ratings downgrade and so increase the cost of past debt as well as impose political costs. Partial commonwealth funding would ease this problem. The matching loans would be on the commonwealth's balance sheet alone, but would be serviced by the state. Guarantees of servicing the loans could be made by securing them against general purpose grants.

The matching loans would be available whether the state was managing infrastructure projects directly or through the private sector. In the latter case, the cost of the project would be lowered to the extent that it is not funded at the higher private-sector discount rate.

WAYS TO IMPROVE HEALTHCARE AND EDUCATION

Health and education services lie within the constitutional authority of the states, but have become joint responsibilities with the commonwealth through the provision of special purpose payments. Health and education are huge industries, comprising approximately 13 per cent of the Australian economy, and almost 20 per cent of jobs. There has been a large increase in public spending on health and education over the past decade or so, but this has not led to a commensurate improvement in outcomes.

In recent years, there has been a productive expansion of independent research on the effectiveness of health programmes, including at the Institute of Applied Economic Research at the University of Melbourne, the Grattan Institute and now the Mitchell Institute. We are in a stronger position to define reform in the public interest and to argue for it against private interests in the health and education sectors than we were a generation ago.

More effective provision of health and education services begins by establishing unambiguous responsibility with one or other level of government. Currently, the main expertise lies within the states. While a precise assessment of productivity is not possible in health and education, the opportunities for improvement can be illustrated quickly. One such opportunity in health is the removal of requirements that highly trained and expensive medical personnel perform tasks that could be done by others with adequate training: the issuance of a medical certificate or a prescription; the exclusive role of doctors in the administration of routine vaccinations; the restricted role of paramedics as first responders to situations where early intervention would yield the greatest benefit; and underinvestment in preventive interventions.

In health, there are significant gains to be made simply by raising the performance of lagging states. In public hospitals, it is said that New South Wales and Queensland would each save about $1 billion per annum if they operated at Victorian levels of efficiency. There are large opportunities for more effective provision of health services by shifting the emphasis from treating disease to prevention. Important gains have already been made since health insurers were allowed to invest in preventive actions in order to reduce costs. More generally, there are opportunities for improving health outcomes cost-effectively by shifting a proportion of health dollars from the hospital to the primary-health sector.

The ageing of the population alongside improvements in medical technology have led to decisions at the beginning and end of life taking on large economic as well as moral consequences. It is thought that 10 per cent of total healthcare costs may be incurred at the end of life on interventions that recipients would prefer not to have done.

In education, current research emphasises the critical importance of teacher quality: it is essential to improve the quality of training and to create incentives to keep the best teachers in the system. There has been much emphasis on reducing class sizes over the past generation. Class sizes are a significant driver of costs. International studies suggest that higher salaries to retain more of the best teachers would be more cost-effective in improving education outcomes than smaller classes.

While there are apparently straightforward opportunities for improvement, reform must find a way through complex political and policy processes. During the long booms, political parties have responded to demands for better health and education with promises of higher spending – and they continued to do so in 2013. Health and education costs are mainly labour, with a low import component, so the real depreciation that is at the core of Australia's adjustment to the end of the boom will reduce real costs in international currency without any cutting of programmes. But improved effectiveness in service delivery is going to be critical to maintaining quality and providing for the aged.

Any effective reform of health or education will have to deal with the powerful forces of 'provider capture', and the ability of private interests to mobilise resources in defence of the status quo. Short timeframes are imposed on decision-making by the electoral cycle and are at odds with the time required for the benefits of reform to be realised; private interest groups have become increasingly effective at exploiting this mismatch. The political influence of the doctors' unions and pharmaceutical organisations is legendary, and other healthcare and teaching groups are not averse to exerting industrial and political pressure.

There are measurement gaps in health and education. A related problem is that of 'information asymmetries': in a market economy where we increasingly rely on the rational and 'optimising' behaviour of the individual, the consumers of health and education are unable to act in this way because they lack the information that providers have. Public mechanisms for provision of information need to be developed if a larger role for market mechanisms is to lead to better outcomes. The national assessment programme for literacy and numeracy that was introduced in 2008 is a model for commonwealth information services to assist informed choices.

There appear to be some straightforward opportunities for lowering costs without lowering the quality of services, but none can be taken up without the public interest prevailing in a fierce contest of ideas. The opportunity for vested industrial and other interests to play one level of government against the other is fatal for efforts to improve effectiveness.

Ending ambiguity in responsibility within the Federation is the first requirement for more effective services. If the commonwealth is better placed to manage hospitals, let it be given responsibility to do so. But if such a change in the division of powers within our Federation is judged not to be desirable or possible, let us have no ambiguity about responsibility lying with the states.

Health and education are especially well suited to competitive federalism, with states and territories seeking to establish in the eyes of their electorates that they are more effective than others in delivering services. The essential commonwealth role is to establish minimum national standards and norms, to measure performance, and to allow residents of different parts of our Federation to measure the effectiveness of services against the best Australian and international practice.

FEDERAL REFORM AND THE END OF THE BOOM

The big resources states, Western Australia and Queensland, face severe fiscal pressures as their royalty income is equalised away by the Grants Commission just as it is falling. The downgrading in the credit rating of the WA government in September 2013 was a reflection of this pressure. The sum of the budget deficits of the states and territories in the years immediately ahead would be recognised as being of large national significance if all were measured in the same way as the commonwealth's. The states cannot fund deficits as readily and at such low cost as the commonwealth, so we will probably be dealing with severe fiscal problems of the Federation. Weakness in one part of it will generate problems and costs for every part. The challenge will be to manage short-term problems in ways that are consistent with long-term reforms.

The commonwealth government's decisions following the review of federal relations proposed by the prime minister would be placed before a premiers' council-type forum to consider reform of the Federation. From the beginning, the prime minister could make it clear that he was working towards a package of new arrangements to be implemented from some distant date, such as 2020 – long enough in the future for short-term political calculations not to dominate each head of government's perspectives. A Long-Term List of federal financial reforms, like the Long-Term List of productivity-raising reforms discussed in Chapter 6, would underpin confidence in Australia's growth prospects. From now till 2020 seems a long time, but it is nevertheless shorter than the time in office of prime ministers who have presided over Australian governments for over three-fifths of the time since Federation. The new prime minister can reasonably aspire to being around to experience the fruits of his labours in office, and not only as a historic legacy.

CHAPTER 9
AVOIDING DANGEROUS CLIMATE CHANGE

Around 250 years ago, the onset of modern economic development added a new component to climate change on Earth: human activity leading to the partial return to the atmosphere of carbon that had been sequestered in living things and in the Earth's crust through natural processes. The clearing of forests and woodlands for agriculture and, above all, the combustion of fossil carbon began to raise the atmospheric proportion of carbon dioxide and other greenhouse gases. These processes became larger and faster after World War II, and again in the Platinum Age of the early twenty-first century.

While modern physics recognised in theory the warming effect of carbon dioxide and other 'greenhouse gases' from the late nineteenth century, only since the 1980s have scientists understood the empirical relationships between ongoing economic growth and warming well enough to be confident about suggesting strong action. By the early 1990s, there was international agreement on the need to reduce the dangers of human-induced climate change. It was then widely thought that most of the world's greenhouse gas emissions would continue to be generated in the old industrial countries for a considerable period. There would be time later for developed countries to take early action and for the developing countries to join the mitigation effort.

But the same Chinese economic growth that gave Australia its resources boom also accelerated the increase in atmospheric greenhouse gases. In the early twenty-first century, the Chinese, Indian and Indonesian economies were growing strongly – they were the world's most populous developing countries. All three were at stages of development in which economic growth was particularly energy-intensive. And for all of them, coal was a relatively low-cost source of energy, if environmental problems were ignored. Unless action was taken to break the link between economic growth and emissions, China would account for 41 per cent of global emissions in 2030, and India for 11 per cent. Major interventions were required.

A SUCCESSFUL APPROACH TO MITIGATION

Early international meetings sought binding agreements to reduce carbon emissions. The Copenhagen meeting in

December 2009 showed that there would be no early comprehensive and binding agreement. The development of an alternative was led by President Barack Obama and the heads of government of four large developing countries: China, India, Brazil and South Africa. I call the new approach, which was formally adopted at Cancún in December 2010, 'concerted unilateral mitigation'.

For the time being, each country specifies unilaterally and voluntarily its emissions targets – developed countries as absolute reductions and developing countries as reductions in emissions intensity or against business as usual. These can be calibrated by each country's assessment of the progress of others. They are serious domestic commitments communicated to the international community. In 2015, a Paris conference will seek a comprehensive binding agreement, to come into effect in 2020.

But whatever the outcome in Paris, it is now clear that concerted unilateral mitigation can take us a considerable way. The domestic targets at Cancún represented large reductions from business as usual for the developed and major developing countries alike. The European Union and Japan – already with emissions per person much less than half those in Australia, the United States and Canada – all made commitments to go much lower. The European Union unconditionally committed to cutting emissions by 20 per cent on 1990 levels by 2020, and by 30 per cent if others made commensurate efforts. Japan undertook to reduce emissions by 25 per cent on 1990 levels.

The world's two largest emitters of greenhouse gases, China and the United States, had previously declined to make commitments, but in 2009 they both announced major departures from their established trajectories. These were presented formally to the United Nations in 2010.

China said that it would reduce the emissions intensity of its economic activity by 40–45 per cent between 2005 and 2020, at the same time as implementing an unprecedentedly large programme of reforestation. The United States announced that it would reduce emissions by 17 per cent on 2005 levels by 2020.

The commitments under concerted unilateral mitigation were probably more ambitious than they would have been in a notionally legally binding agreement negotiated by all countries. Formal negotiations make country representatives defensive. This explains the paradox of trade negotiations: formal negotiations to reduce trade barriers often lead to less trade liberalisation than unilateral decisions in a national frame.

So far almost all substantial countries are making strong progress on their undertakings. The European Union has introduced many simultaneous measures: renewable energy targets; feed-in tariffs for various forms of renewable energy; fiscal subsidies, including for carbon capture and storage and nuclear developments; carbon taxes; and an EU-wide Emissions Trading Scheme (ETS). Permit prices under the ETS have ranged from well above $A40 to as low as $A5 (they were $A7.72 on 19

September 2013). Low recent prices reflect weak domestic growth, which means that the other interventions can deliver the required reduction in emissions without much help from the ETS. Higher prices would return with stronger economic growth or tighter targets. They would cause the trading scheme to take more of the mitigation load, and at some price make each of the detailed interventions redundant.

Japan was making good progress towards its target before the Fukushima disaster reduced the role of nuclear power, but has become less confident of meeting its target since then.

MUSCULAR DIRECT ACTION IN THE UNITED STATES

President George W. Bush said in 2007 that US emissions would reach a peak in 2025 and then fall. We now know that US emissions peaked in the year in which Bush was speaking and President Obama's 2020 target is within reach.

When Obama revealed the 17 per cent cut in 2009, he had intended that an ETS would be the main instrument for cutting emissions. A bill for such a scheme passed the House of Representatives in 2010, but a vote in the Senate was avoided by filibuster. The Congress after the 2010 elections would not support carbon-pricing legislation.

In a personal conversation early in 2011, the US secretary for energy, Stephen Chu, advised me that while the government would have liked to have met its international commitments in an efficient and low-cost manner through an ETS, it would now meet its targets through other means. He described how an inter-agency process had estimated the social cost of carbon at a bit over $US20 per tonne, rising over time. This price would guide the development of regulations for reducing emissions from all of the main sources, including electricity generation, transport, appliances and buildings. In a major speech on climate change in mid-2013, President Obama brought together the outcomes of far-reaching developments in regulation and other steps to reduce emissions.

Many measures have contributed to cutting US emissions: state and federal environmental regulations and energy-efficiency schemes; harassment of the coal and some other fossil fuel industries by non-government agencies; state and federal support for renewable and nuclear energy; regulatory requirements for use of renewable energy; and emissions trading schemes in some states. This is muscular direct action. The largest of the emissions trading schemes – in California and some other western states, and linked to the Canadian province of Quebec – came into operation in January 2013. The federal government will not regulate emissions as severely in states that have effective emissions trading schemes.

Over the past several years, emissions reduction in power generation in the United States has been reinforced by low natural gas prices. Gas prices have fallen dramatically, driven by the combination of large new reserves and restrictions on exports. While it has been accepted for some time that there would be no substantial new coal-based electricity generators in the United States – and the president's policy outlaws them without carbon capture and storage – the low gas prices are driving the closure of much established capacity.

The big falls in US gas prices are in contrast to the Australian experience, although our east coast has had proportionately much larger increases in gas resources than the United States. As discussed in Chapter 6, our trade policies have made all the difference. Australia has allowed free exports, and gas prices are in the process of increasing by two or three times, up to export parity prices. Some Australian interests favour a partial version of the US restriction on exports, among other things to assist gas in competition with coal for environmental reasons. Viewed as a means of bringing down emissions (by replacing coal), restrictions on gas exports would be extremely expensive, as they have been in the United States.

The US experience shows that regulatory action can bring emissions down a long way. It also shows that to do this, direct action must be muscular and intrusive, and expensive.

CHINA'S RAPID PROGRESS

China, too, is seeing many regulatory and fiscal interventions. Smaller and environmentally and economically inefficient coal-based electricity generators have been forced to close, replaced by super-hypercritical plants operating at the world frontier of low-emissions intensity. So too have environmentally inefficient metals smelting and other industrial plants. Renewables and nuclear power have been favoured by subsidies, high feed-in tariffs and regulatory purchase requirements. There has been high investment to make the national electricity grid more flexible in absorbing large quantities of inflexible (nuclear) and intermittent (wind and solar) sources of power. There is much money for research, development and the commercialisation of low-emissions technologies. Trials of emissions trading are being conducted in seven cities and two provinces as steps towards a national scheme if things go well. Large regulatory pressure and fiscal subsidies are driving increased efficiency in energy use for households and business.

In August 2013, the Chinese government made renewable energy and energy efficiency the main focus of fiscal expansion, when the economic growth rate was threatening to fall below the 7 per cent established as the desirable lower limit. The increased spending in the 2013 stimulus package exceeds half the total budget expansion in response to the Great Crash of 2008. China now is investing more than any other country in all of the low-emissions sources of electricity: hydro-electric, wind, nuclear, solar, bio-mass. It expects to succeed Germany as the world's largest producer of solar energy over the next year. China is also the centre of the largest research and development drive on carbon capture and storage. It is making an immense effort to increase the efficiency with which energy is used.

China is also seeking to reduce emissions from transport. It is doing two big things. The Chinese government has given electrified intra-urban and intercity rail high priority in planning. This has survived the general downgrading in priority of infrastructure investment since 2011. And China has promoted the fully electric car through consumer and producer subsidies, and has announced a target of having 5 million vehicles on the road by 2020. This is likely to provide large scale and low costs in electric-car manufacturing earlier than in other countries. The fuel efficiency standards for conventional automobiles are being revised in line with emerging norms in advanced developed countries.

After annual growth near double digits for a decade, electricity generation increased by only 5.7 per cent (well below the GDP growth rate) in 2012. Almost the whole of the increase was contributed by hydro-electric, wind and nuclear, in that order, with solar growing even more rapidly from a much smaller basis. Emissions from the electricity sector declined a bit in 2012. This tendency seems to have continued: total coal use in China (domestic production plus imports) was a bit over 3 per cent lower in the first half of 2013 than in the corresponding period of 2012.

LARGE REDUCTIONS BUT A LONG WAY TO GO

Developed and major developing countries generally have been making good progress towards their domestic Cancún commitments at lower costs than had been anticipated.

It is not possible to convert such commitments into a precise assessment of likely implications for global temperatures, as we do not know what is going to happen next. Despite recent progress, a marked acceleration is necessary to avoid risks of warming of 4 degrees or more. However, Chinese and global progress in lowering the growth path of emissions has kept open the possibility of meeting the 2 degrees objective.

If that is to occur, global emissions need to fall by more than half by the middle of the century, to an average of no more than 2 tonnes per person, and to keep falling after that. This has to occur in a world with expectations in many developing countries, containing most of the world's people, that their standards of living will keep rising towards those in the world's developed countries. The arithmetic says that developed countries on average will have to reduce emissions absolutely by more than 90 per cent. That means close to zero emissions for electricity generation and transport, and large reductions elsewhere.

AUSTRALIA BENEFITS BY DOING ITS FAIR SHARE

Australia would suffer more than other developed countries by a failure of climate change mitigation. It is in Australia's national interest for the world to succeed. It is in Australia's interest to encourage international efforts by doing our fair share.

If the world has to reduce emissions by more than half by the middle of the century, and developed countries by over 90 per cent, what is Australia's fair share? The international community has decided that what matters is reducing actual emissions, whatever the cost and whatever the motive.

It is immensely to Australia's advantage that the United Nations has decided to calculate actual emissions for each country with reference to tradeable entitlements rather than emissions within a country's boundaries. Australia's economic structure leads to relatively large emissions per person, so it is advantageous for us to buy entitlements from places that are able to reduce emissions at a lower cost.

So what is Australia's fair share? The Climate Change Authority has been established to provide independent and transparent advice on this matter. It takes account of what others are doing. It insulates the development of advice on emissions targets from the raw political process. Over time it could take its place as an important independent element of our system of economic governance, alongside the Reserve Bank and the Productivity Commission. The new Coalition government would find the work of such an authority helpful.

My own recommendation in the 2008 Climate Change Review had unconditional and conditional elements. I said that Australia should reduce emissions unconditionally by 5 per cent on 2000 levels by 2020. This is what we would do in the absence of other countries taking action to reduce emissions. We should be prepared to go further, up to a 25 per cent reduction, in the event of effective international action. The Labor government, with the support of the Opposition, adopted these targets. The unconditional and conditional targets were reaffirmed during the 2013 election campaign by the Coalition. In 2010, the conditional Australian commitments to the United Nations were given precise form. Our emissions would be reduced by 15 per cent if other developed countries took on comparable commitments and major developing countries committed to substantially restraining emissions. They would be reduced by 25 per cent in the context of a comprehensive global agreement capable of meeting the 2 degrees objective.

Other countries' efforts already would seem to trigger Australia's commitment to a 15 per cent reduction. This is similar to the commitment that the United States has made and towards which it is making solid progress. The comparison is relevant, since the US also has high energy use per person, high fossil fuel use and strong population growth through immigration. To meet Australia's bipartisan policy communicated to the United Nations, we will need to go further still if a new and deeper set of commitments is made by others at Paris in 2015.

Chapter 6 notes that Australia's economy has already been affected by climate change. Climate change-induced falls in productivity were experienced in utilities and agriculture. It can be expected to be increasingly important in the future, even with effective global mitigation and good fortune in holding temperature increases to 2 degrees. It will be overwhelmingly important if the international effort has incomplete success and future Australians have to live with temperature increases of more than 2 degrees. Adaptation is a useful if expensive accompaniment to prevention but not an alternative to it: it is fanciful to think of nation-states in their current form surviving temperature increases of 4 degrees or more. The costs of climate change and adaptation are part of our current economic reality and will grow at an uncomfortable pace in the decades ahead.

WHICH APPROACH IS CHEAPER?

While the former Labor and the current Coalition governments concur on targets, their approaches to meeting them are radically different. How we get there is not important to the climate outcome, but it does have implications for productivity and the budget.

Modelling in the 2008 Climate Change Review and subsequently by the Treasury suggests that Australia doing its fair share in a global effort to hold the temperature increase to 2 degrees would shave about one-tenth of a percentage point from growth each year until 2050. However, within about half a century the gains from avoided climate change – the gains from Australia doing its fair share of the global effort – would exceed the costs of mitigation. These gains over losses would grow larger and larger over time.

Part of the cost of global mitigation to Australian incomes comes from export prices falling as other countries do their fair share. The collapse of growth in China's burning of coal for power in 2011 has already contributed to much lower thermal coal prices. The costs to Australia of the Chinese (and American) movement away from coal-based electricity is much greater than it needed to be because we kept investing in new capacity when the writing was on the wall. Billions of dollars of investment has been written down and written off since the market changed after 2011.

Experience in many countries shows that cutting emissions is getting cheaper and proceeding more rapidly than once anticipated. The cost of solar photovoltaic panels made in China in at least one major plant that I have inspected twice has fallen by 90 per cent over the past five years.

Like Europe, the United States and China, Australia has large numbers of minor policies that have contributed something to cutting emissions, but these are largely overshadowed by the Renewable Energy Target established in 2010, and the Clean Energy package with a national ETS as its centrepiece in 2011.

The Renewable Energy Target requires an increasing proportion of electricity to come from large-scale renewable projects, rising to an amount, fixed by legislation, that was estimated to be 20 per cent by 2020. Unexpected falls in electricity demand make it likely that renewables will fulfil more than a quarter of total requirements by 2020. The combination of the Renewable Energy Target and greater efficiency in electricity use is leading to substantially more rapid decarbonisation of electricity generation than I contemplated in the 2008 Review. It is also leading to lower wholesale power prices as renewable energy competes with established coal-based electricity for a declining market. This is an unanticipated but large benefit for consumers of electricity.

The ETS that came into effect in July 2012 requires all large-scale emitters of greenhouse gases to surrender a permit for each tonne of carbon dioxide-equivalent released into the atmosphere. Permits are made available at a fixed price through the first three years. From July 2015 they will be sold by auction or can be purchased from participants in the European emissions trading system.

The Australian scheme raises substantial revenue. About half is returned to households as tax cuts and social security increases, and the remainder paid as compensation to business (falling over time) and support for development of renewable energy.

After being on a strongly increasing trajectory for many years, Australian emissions have stabilised under the new policies. Emissions from the electricity sector fell by more than 7 per cent over the year to June 2013. The scheme has made enterprises much more aware of emissions and opportunities for reducing them. This has been especially important in containing what is in any case rapid growth in 'fugitive emissions' associated with coal mining and gas production and processing. Care is taken now to use technologies that involve lower emissions because high emissions could become costly at a later time.

Current policies can meet the more and more demanding reductions that Australia is likely to be called to make, at a relatively low cost and with minimal political discretion and business uncertainty. For a considerable time, the current arrangements are likely to be an economically efficient, large and increasing source of revenue as compensation payments to coal-based generators cease in 2014–15, as compensation to trade-exposed industries is reviewed by the Productivity Commission from 2015, and as international carbon prices rise with economic recovery in the European Union and the tightening of targets in Europe, Australia and beyond.

The Coalition government came to power in 2013 committed to removing the carbon price. It would seek to meet the established targets by Direct Action, to which it has allocated a sum of money and says there will be no more.

I have no reason to doubt the sincerity of the prime minister and his environment minister in telling the Australian people before the election that the nation's emissions targets would be met under a Coalition government. The environment minister explicitly embraced the conditional as well as the unconditional targets. Since taking office, he has noted that strong progress on emissions is being made in the United States and especially China.

Direct Action, in principle, allows Australia to meet the commitments to the United Nations that were made by the government with the then Opposition's support. However, on the evidence currently available, it is hard to see how the amount of money allocated to Direct Action would be anywhere near enough for us to meet the unconditional target. Using Direct Action to meet a 15 or 25 per cent reduction from 2000 levels by 2020 would be much more difficult still. As the United States and China have shown, it is possible to make radical changes in emissions trajectories without carbon pricing. As the United States and China have also shown, large emissions reductions through Direct Action require expensive muscular interventions of a kind not yet discussed by the Coalition. Of course, the government can change the content of Direct Action to meet the 2020 commitments, but it would be more expensive to concentrate cuts into a short period than to achieve them gradually.

Australia's trade-exposed and emissions-intensive industries are thoroughly protected under the current arrangements. To comprehensively replace these arrangements with other measures generating similar emissions reductions would not increase incentives for economic activity and may reduce them.

Coal mining is less protected than other trade-exposed industries under current policies, with the average cost of purchasing permits at about 50 cents per tonne in 2013 after deducting assistance from the carbon-pricing scheme. This has been the source of considerable opposition to carbon pricing from the coal industry, supported by mining and industry more broadly. To keep the issue in perspective, the net cost of Australian carbon pricing to coal mining represents much less than 1 per cent of the revenue loss from the fall in international prices from 2011 to 2013, and less than 5 per cent of the gain from the fall in the dollar between March and September 2013. The costs of permits to coal mining, as for other business, would fall by two-thirds with the link to Europe in 2014 or 2015, if European prices remained at their current levels.

The Coalition envisages retaining elements of existing policy under the rubric of Direct Action. There is bipartisan support for the Renewable Energy Target, which will be the main source of emissions cuts in the electricity sector until the European–Australian carbon price rises considerably. The government is committed to retaining the Australian Renewable Energy Agency, which provides support for innovation in low-emissions technologies. Modification of the former government's Carbon Farming Initiative can be seen as an element of Direct Action. Carbon pricing interacts productively with each of these ways of reducing emissions.

The new government has placed considerable emphasis on the potential for sequestration of carbon in soils, woodlands and forests. Prime Minister Abbott has often named my work as an authority for his statements about meeting Australia's targets in this way. It is worth putting much effort into technology for measurement and sequestration, and into leading the international community into wider recognition of its contribution. It has to be recognised, however, that these are early days, and that for soil and woodlands we are talking about technical possibilities rather than certain, internationally recognised methods to reduce emissions.

Other Direct Action measures to which the minister for environment has alluded also have potential for curbing emissions, although we do not know how much and at what cost. The most productive of these could be brought within the framework of the established system, where they would be funded by part of the revenue generated by carbon pricing.

The new government is bound by its election commitments to introduce legislation to remove carbon pricing. That legislation will pass the House of Representatives. If the legislation were to succeed in the Senate, it would deepen the budgetary problems with which the government will eventually have to deal. It would lead to larger sacrifices of productivity than would be necessary with broadly based carbon pricing. It would lead either to much higher costs later in the decade or to Australia breaching its commitments to the international community and damaging its own interest in the global mitigation effort. And it would set the Australian polity on another long journey to find a way to make our contribution to combating global climate change, distracting the government and the polity from the great economic challenges facing Australia.

It would be a victory that the government may come to wish it had not won.

PART 3

CHAPTER 10
A CHANGED POLITICAL CULTURE

Since the bursting of the debt-funded bubble in 2008, democratic capitalism has been having its hardest time since the Great Depression and World War II. Ours is one of a small number of developed countries so far to have escaped great economic difficulties and profound doubts about the social and political order. Australia's continued success is important for the welfare of Australians, and also for the standing of democratic capitalism in a changing world.

Australia will only avoid the problems of other developed countries if we manage our own challenges well. We will be tested by the end of the China resources boom.

Before discussing recent changes in the political culture here, let us recollect some of the lessons of modern economic development. The immense achievements of economic growth arose from a melding of capacity for collective action with the energy and genius of individuals and small groups. As social scientists have sought explanations for why some societies succeed economically and others fail, they have kept coming back to getting the balance right between collective institutions and the constraints on and incentives for people to pursue private interests.

In early 1989, an American political scientist wrote an influential article that was later developed into a book called *The End of History*. History, or the later and important part of it, had been a struggle among ideas about how economic and political life should be ordered. History had ended with the triumph of democratic capitalism.

The author, Francis Fukuyama, has recently published an article called 'The Future of History'. He now says that the future of democratic capitalism depends on whether powerful internal tendencies to wider inequality and the influence of wealth in the democratic process can be contained and corrected.

Moral philosophers and sociologists have long drawn attention to the social underpinnings of modern economic and political institutions. Capitalism stands on the shoulders of a pre-capitalist ideology – a system of beliefs and moral precepts that constrains the greed and ambitions of individuals in areas where they will be damaging to order and prosperity, but allows them loose rein where this is productive for society as a whole. But the widening scope of the market economy corrodes old constraints. The democratic capitalist order is in trouble unless we renew old or build alternative sources of constraint on individual ambition and greed, and do so in a way that retains the dynamism of individual initiative expressed through the market.

These moral and social constraints make it possible for people to accept personally unsatisfactory outcomes from political processes – in contrast with recent developments in democratic Egypt.

They make possible a system of general taxation that can support a functioning state – a system that would not lead to widespread tax evasion and the bankruptcy of the state, as it did in Greece.

They mean that leaders forgo opportunities to enrich themselves through their offices. The failure of development in many of the world's poor countries – indeed, concerns about stability even in the more successful developing economies – demonstrate the consequences of weaknesses in restraint.

They mean that limits are placed on the use of corporate wealth to exercise power over policy in a democracy. The extreme deregulation of the North Atlantic financial systems, the Great Crash of 2008 and the loss of five years of potential growth in much of the developed world show the importance of such factors to the world's most developed economies.

Remove these constraints, and we have broken the foundations of modern economic development and democratic capitalism.

None of the big inflexion points in human history came from the blueprint of a thinker or leader. Adam Smith's *The Wealth of Nations* emerged from his observation of the creative power of markets. Smith helped us to understand the great changes in the currents of history that were occurring in his lifetime, and others were then able to ride those currents further.

We learn for sure that we have reached an inflexion point only when it has passed into history. Once we observe that things have gone wrong, it is usually too late to change course without large disruption and cost. Democratic capitalism may be at such an inflexion point now. Today's big risks are mainly to do with developments in our political culture.

These are issues we should keep in mind as we think about whether and, if so, how Australia can maintain full employment and high (if for a while somewhat lower) living standards after the China resources boom.

THE POLITICAL CULTURE OF THE DOG DAYS

Prime Minister Julia Gillard and Treasurer Wayne Swan did a fair job of economic policy after the China boom reached its peak and started its long downward slide in 2011, but they were judged by the electorate to have failed. That's what Dog Days do. People had come to expect rising employment, incomes and services, along with falling taxes, but the economy could no longer support these.

Governments look bad in the Dog Days. The former government's position looked worse because its revenue forecasts were consistently too high. The largest of the six-monthly upgrades to the budget deficit came out three days before the calling of the 2013 election. The government had accepted official advice, as a good government should, and paid a high price in credibility.

Dog Days end when people abandon expectations of rising living standards and accept that some of the private gains of the Salad Days must be surrendered for the common good. This only happens in a timely way if leaders explain that times have changed and outline a programme of shared restraint. Otherwise the alignment of expectations with reality is a long slog, usually involving recession, massive business failures and high unemployment.

We seemed to be making a start on lowering expectations in the May 2013 budget, when some measures created losers and the Opposition did not come out against them. That ground was lost in August, when a modest measure to remove an income tax loophole was attacked by the private interests affected by it and rejected by the Opposition, and then became prominent in the election campaign. The Opposition also gave prominence to an extraordinary piece of middle-class welfare, its paid parental-leave scheme. These developments cancelled the budget message that the good times might have stopped rolling.

During the election campaign, the former government made slight reference to the challenge of transition from the China resources boom but said nothing about what needed to be done in response. The Opposition said that it would stop the boom from ending and would solve the budget problem because improved confidence on its election would lead to stronger economic growth.

We are in the Dog Days for some time yet – for years, if we have no effective leadership. Excellent economic policy will look ordinary, and ordinary policy abominable. Good policy has to begin with a huge readjustment of community expectations. But a changed political culture presents political leaders with an awful choice: between easy short-term political gains from telling the electorate what it wants to hear, and the risk inherent in explaining and seeking to advance the public interest.

A NEW MEDIA CULTURE MAKES GOOD POLICY HARDER

A massive technological change in communications took effect from the late 1980s and accelerated through the early twenty-first century. It has reshaped the way people exchange information and changed the nature of politics.

One early consequence was the expansion of the influence of national media, both print and electronic. The *Financial Review* and the *Australian* had both been around since the first half of the 1960s, but they became more truly national. This was on the whole supportive of a government with a national reform agenda. It strengthened national against state governments, just as it fostered the development of national leagues in all of the main sporting codes.

In parallel with the expansion of the national media, the News Ltd purchase of the Herald and Weekly Times group in 1987 brought over 60 per cent of the ownership of Australian newspapers under single control. This introduced monopoly in media ownership to an unprecedented extent among the substantial democracies. Such single control of print media would generally be problematic in a democracy even without the major shareholder being a citizen of a foreign country and having a well-earned reputation for opinionated political activism. The approval of the takeover was a mistake of the Reform Era that casts a long shadow.

A second change in media culture came with the increased use of the internet for classified advertisements. The classifieds had been local natural monopolies of the daily broadsheets with high reputations, most importantly the *Sydney Morning Herald* and the *Age*. Revenue from them generated rents that were used, among other things, to subsidise high-quality journalism and the training of journalists. The rise of the internet eroded these monopolies, which in turn weakened the broadsheets' ability to focus on long-term issues and undertake deeper analysis.

The third change came with the increasing role of the electronic media as information sources. The new technologies underwrote the emergence of continuous news channels and a proliferation of current affairs programmes.

The entry costs to the new media were low, so internet news sources became much more important.

These developments saw the emergence of the '24-hour news cycle'. A simple and bold political statement would receive instantaneous and wide coverage, but would not sustain interest for long enough to require an elaborate defence. Superficiality was no disadvantage. The clear negative statement was much more likely to be heard. Political leaders were taken more seriously if they continuously generated new messages. To compete with the constantly changing news on the 24-hour cycle, newspapers, too, were encouraged into the sensational, the ephemeral and the negative.

The authority of the broadsheets declined, and with it their role as arbiters of what was worth a place in the national conversation. The polls tell us that only the public broadcaster, the Australian Broadcasting Corporation, enhanced its credibility.

The decline in commitment to accuracy and balanced reporting has gone furthest in the News Ltd (now News Corp Australia) majority of newspapers. I was able to observe this most clearly in relation to the reporting of climate change. Errors of fact brought to the attention of journalists were generally no longer corrected (although some individual journalists maintained higher professional standards).

There was a systematic selection of material for publication in the newspapers, so that readers who relied on these sources of information were exposed to an unrepresentative subset of reality. This was important, for example, in the reporting of international progress in reducing greenhouse gas emissions, notably in the United States and China.

Over time, newspapers that take this approach to accuracy and balance in reporting lose credibility with the public, so the system may be partially self-correcting as more reliable sources grow in influence. I say *may* not *will*, as it is not certain that the commercial incentives will drive competitors towards accuracy and balance.

The distortion in the reporting of policy and politics in a major part of the print media was an important advantage for Prime Minister Abbott in his thrust for the leadership during the four years to September 2013. It is at best a mixed blessing once in office. All mortals are easily encouraged into deeper error if they are reassured of the wisdom of every proposal that passes their mouths. In 2013, a prominent economic columnist for the *Australian* found reassuring things to say about the economic impact of the paid parental-leave scheme. All good leaders are at times without cover. It is of no advantage for the naked emperor to have courtiers praise the beauty of his clothes.

The proliferation of information sources has led to a fragmentation of the national conversation about policy. People can choose the sources that tell them what they want to hear. This seems to have the effect of entrenching established attitudes.

People can choose their facts. This may have been important in commercial as well as policy discussion. One wonders how influential the selection of sources of information was in the thermal coal investment decisions at the height of the boom – decisions that now have been shown to have wasted many billions of dollars of shareholders' wealth. The absorption of information readily available from other sources (including my climate change reviews) at the time of the investment decisions would have led to caution about the effects of policy developments in China and the United States on prospects for thermal coal.

The proliferation of information sources has a positive side: pluralism, and the opportunity to reach a large audience with a view not supported by the monopolistic print media. Specialist centres of communications can develop more profound analysis and information for niche audiences. Political campaigns can be developed independently of the print media, especially if they are built around single and simple issues.

On the whole, these developments in media culture to date have made the prosecution of a wide-ranging positive reform programme more difficult. In general, they favour an Opposition with a simple negative message over a government seeking to deal with the complex issues that arise when governing in the public interest.

But these are early days. The use of the new opportunities could evolve in a number of ways. It is possible, for example, that the best of the internet media outlets could develop mass audiences that can support investment in high-quality journalism. The greater use of international sources is leading to better information being widely available on foreign policy.

While the new media environment in Australia seems to favour the negative and has done so up till now, we have not yet seen a major effort by a strong political leader to appeal to the electorate through the new media culture on a programme of reform in the public interest. It might be effective.

THE TIMIDITY OF POLITICAL PROFESSIONALS

One large change in political culture has been the rise of professionalism in the careers of leaders and the approach of parties to winning elections. Another is the decline in mass membership parties with strong roots in the community and consistent ideological themes that are widely recognised. These are closely related developments: the decline of the latter has left a vacuum that has been filled by the former, and the advance of professionalism has reduced the appeal to citizens of participation in political parties. The problems and the need for reform are more acute in Labor than in the Coalition.

Parties have become increasingly sophisticated in identifying the marginal and the uncommitted voter, and more focused in election campaigns on appealing to them. The focus is increasingly on the specific and local and mundane and narrow and immediate rather than the grand themes of politics. Policies are distilled to slogans. The focus on the uncommitted encourages caution. This has made election campaigns themselves uninteresting to most citizens who are generally interested in policy and politics.

The truth of the democratic electorate, identified by Cicero more than 2000 years ago, is that voters are more likely to support someone who tells them what they want to hear. Professional polling and politics has confirmed this truth and identified more precisely what it is that voters say they desire. In the short term, at least, leaders are rewarded electorally by repeating back to uncommitted voters the things they have said that they want to hear.

All of these tendencies have been present since the late 1970s, and they expanded in the 1980s when the systematic use of polling with focus groups became important in structuring the positions of political parties and guiding election campaigns. They have become more influential over time, as parties have grown both more expert in the use of the data and more reliant on it.

I have my doubts about the policy effects and also the long-term political value of focus groups and highly professional polling. The messages from focus groups told the Labor Party to abandon the ETS, and then to abandon the prime minister whose electoral fortunes diminished when he accepted this advice. I doubt this was even sound short-term politics.

But these are lonely doubts. For the moment, the focus group and opinion poll loom large in Australian policymaking. For the moment, reform in the public interest cannot prosper unless its proponents change what people want to hear. Leaders of the major political parties, and especially the prime minister, are in the best position to change what people want to hear.

The focus groups and the polling never endorsed the sweeping policy changes of the Reform Era. They are unlikely ever to endorse the policies required for adjustment to the end of the China resources boom. At first sight, this change in Australian political culture seems to be decisively against a new Reform Era.

And yet the previous Reform Era was not blocked by the early rise of the new political professionalism. I was present at a briefing of Prime Minister Hawke by the Labor Party's highly reputed and successful pollster after the 1984 election. (I presume that I had been asked to be present at this particular meeting so that I would learn about the problems that I had created for the prime minister.) The government had won the election comfortably, but had lost ground after a dogged scare campaign by the leader of the Opposition against various measures to tax income that had previously slipped through the net and to tighten eligibility for social security.

'We have got away with this one,' the pollster said, 'but we can't risk any more economic reform.'

The pollster kept thinking about this episode, and later advised that bold reform might even be rewarded by the electorate if accompanied by careful public explanation.

There is no doubt that in the Great Complacency, changes in political and media culture reward leaders who emphasise the negative and tailor their messages to murmurings from the uncommitted middle ground. This has been brilliantly productive from Opposition, in 2007 and with increased force in 2010 and 2013.

And yet, my view is that even in the twenty-first century, political parties and their leaders in government have much more autonomy in policy than the professional wisdom of the political specialists advising them allows. There is immense power in incumbency both when a government is new and when it is old, which can be used to pursue reform in the public interest.

Once the electorate has endorsed a new government and leader, it changes its mind only for a large reason. While conventional wisdom says that a government wears out its welcome simply with the passing of time, there is no empirical basis for this observation. Six Australian governments have won three successive elections (Hughes–Bruce; Lyons–Menzies; Menzies and successors; Fraser; Hawke–Keating; and Howard). Five of the six have won a fourth election. Of the five that have won four elections, 60 per cent have won a fifth.

The most reliable destroyer of the advantages of incumbency is economic dislocation: only once since we have been able to measure this in the modern way has a government won re-election after a recession. And seen in historical perspective, that sole victory, of Keating in 1993, looks like a postponement of retribution until the Liberal Party found an acceptable programme.

The departure of the electoral dynastic founder greatly weakens the advantages of incumbency. The standing of a prime minister is not easily transferred to a successor within the same party – no successor in office other than Bruce in the 1920s has won more than one election as prime minister. But incumbency with the dynastic founder cannot last forever: sooner or later a leader dies (Lyons, Curtin), finds something more rewarding to do (Barton, Fisher), repudiates or loses the support of colleagues (Hughes Two, Hawke, Rudd One), or decides that he has had enough (Menzies Two). A new leader might as well put the power of incumbency to good use while she has it.

Only once in the thirty-nine federal elections of the past hundred years has government passed from one party to another at an election without a recession or change of prime minister. History will get around to asking deeper questions about the achievement of Kevin Rudd in 2007, when a dynastic founder – John Howard – was toppled for the first time without a recession. Was the challenger unusually attractive to the electorate at the time? Or was the new political culture teaching us that things have changed and incumbency no longer means as much?

When prime ministers with standing in the electorate take strong positions on economic reform in the public interest, they carry a considerable proportion of the electorate with them. An outstanding example is the response to the Whitlam Labor government's 25 per cent across-the-board tariff cut in July 1973. The standing of the prime minister was high in his first year of office. The electorate was strongly supportive of the established policy of high protection, Labor Party supporters more so than others. The tariff cut was dropped on the community without explanation or warning, and yet it received immediate majority support, higher among supporters of the government.

It is the initial reaction of the electorate that is instructive. The persistent criticism from the Opposition and campaigns from private interests who stood to lose began to bite deeply, but only when unemployment rose a year later and the reputation of the government for competence was waning for other reasons.

Non-Labor governments have had the greater longevity. There have been five long-term (three or more terms) non-Labor governments and only one long-term Labor government. This reflects an electoral advantage in conservatism, in the sense of defending the status quo and resisting change. As Machiavelli explained to the Medici princes, reform excites the passions of all who will be hurt by it, but the enthusiasm of no beneficiaries. It is conservatism in the sense of resisting change that is important, rather than in the sense of supporting wealth and capital. Here, the contemporary Labor Party is at least as conservative as the Coalition – although to the extent that Labor conservatism reflects a defence of the traditional role of trade unions in the political order rather than a defence of Australian egalitarianism, it has other electoral disadvantages.

In any case, not doing much is not the answer when business as usual is likely to see a conservative government presiding over economic dislocation. This is the dilemma of the Abbott Coalition government.

KEEPING BAD PROMISES CAN DAMAGE GOOD GOVERNMENT

Tony Abbott as Opposition leader gave the honouring of election promises an unprecedented priority in his criticism of Prime Minister Gillard over the 'carbon tax'. In truth, there is a complex relationship between leaders' standing and the extent to which they honour election commitments.

Both the Whitlam and Hawke governments had to deal with huge changes in circumstances from those that had seemed to face them immediately before they took office. Whitlam was elected on an elaborate programme to expand public services of various kinds. As the global post-war boom came to an abrupt end and Australia's terms of trade fell sharply from late 1973, Whitlam continued to deliver on his promises. This counted for little in the electorate. The government was judged harshly for its failure to meet expectations on full employment.

Hawke took into government the lesson of the Whitlam experience: a determination to meet election commitments after circumstances have changed is economically damaging and politically unwise. Following advice from the Treasury that the budget deficit would be far larger than had been revealed to the public, Hawke immediately set out to cut spending and strengthen revenue in order to make way for a considerably trimmed-down version of Labor's election promises. The voters demonstrated over several elections that they valued the larger and broader commitments to rising employment and economic growth more highly than the truncations of expenditure.

There are counter-examples. The Fraser Coalition government promised a large income tax cut in the 1977 election campaign and put it aside after the election. This was an important factor in corroding the government's standing.

In 1993, the Opposition leader, John Hewson, promised to introduce a goods and services tax, part of which would be used to fund a cut in income tax. The Keating Labor government responded by promising to match the income tax cut without the goods and services tax. But neither the treasurer, John Dawkins, nor the government recovered from the partial withdrawal of these promised cuts after Labor was re-elected.

Prime Minister Gillard's statement before the 2010 election that there would be no 'carbon tax' under a government that she led was lethally damaging in the hands of an effective Opposition leader.

Prime Minister John Howard's distinction between 'core' and 'non-core' promises – made in explaining budget cuts after the 1996 election – was much derided at the time, but a way out of the dilemma that arises when election commitments don't add up to a reasonable response to realities as they reveal themselves in office.

The Abbott Coalition government has been elected with an unusually severe problem of reconciling election commitments with the realities of its time in government. The promise to retain compensation for the ETS, but to repeal the scheme that provides the revenue for this, has repeated the 1993 Keating tactic on matching an opponent's promises on tax cuts.

The expedient of distinguishing between 'core' and 'non-core' elements is not so readily available to Prime Minister Abbott, who, like Whitlam before him, has made a great deal of his commitment to keep all promises to the electorate. The highest-profile promises, and therefore the hardest to put aside as 'non-core', happen to be those that – at best – will make Australia's adjustment more difficult. These include the repeal of the mining tax and ETS, the preservation of the income tax loophole related to the private use of company motor vehicles, and the world's most generous parental-leave scheme. Strong commitments were also made during the election campaign to avoid cuts to any of the major commonwealth programmes: pensions, defence, health and education. At least the commitment to increase defence spending greatly had no timetable attached to it. Most difficult of all for the government will be the high profile given to assurances that economic growth will be greater under a Coalition government and that this will ease pressure on the budget. As Whitlam discovered, the electorate ends up valuing general promises of prosperity more highly than the minutiae of taxation and expenditure.

The Abbott government's postponement until its tenth year of expectations of a surplus has delayed the day of reckoning for its budget contradictions. However, it also removes what had been an important source of budget discipline under the Labor government. All of this means that an effective Opposition leader who emphasises the negative will have plenty to exploit as the gap widens between expectations and emerging realities.

Abbott is the third prime minister of Australia since the Salad Days gave way to Dog Days in 2011. Without strong and early policy action, starting with a transformation of expectations about what the economy can and cannot deliver, the accumulation of economic problems is likely to overwhelm his prime ministership. His task is harder in the political culture of the early twenty-first century.

If he chooses to take strong and early action, he will be able to draw upon an electoral dynastic founder's huge political advantages of incumbency. An effective leader offering strong policy responses that are broadly seen to be equitable is rewarded by the electorate.

Beyond the general advantages of incumbency, the current prime minister has support for the time being from major private interests and from News Corp. The private interests are encouraged that they have a prime minister who agrees with them. Abbott's personal links with News Corp personnel provide him with a reliable praetorian guard, ready to disembowel critics, right or wrong. The support of private interests will be tested, however, as a reform programme designed to deal with Australia's problems must disappoint them. News Corp support will be tested by the limited appeal to media consumers of a positive and complex campaign encouraging restraint in the public interest, and by the competing commercial attractions of simple and negative messages.

The largest of all alterations in political culture through the Great Complacency is the uninhibited entry of corporate wealth directly into the political process, to achieve changes in policy. This has been accompanied by changes in the approach of the business lobbies. Abbott has ridden this tiger into office. His success as prime minister depends on his capacity to put it back in the public-interest cage.

CHAPTER 11
PUBLIC VERSUS PRIVATE INTERESTS

Democratic capitalism has to reconcile great tensions between private interests and the public interest if it is to benefit citizens. These tensions are older than democracy. The risk that they would be resolved against the public interest was once used as an argument by democracy's opponents. The extreme fears of yesteryear have not been realised: modern economic development has had its best days since the advent of democracy. Nevertheless, there is a never-ending contest.

Part 2 outlined a programme of reform that would prevent high unemployment and economic dislocation after the China resources boom. It would be good for the living standards of Australians on average and in general. However, it would also lower the incomes of foreigners and Australians who currently enjoy advantages from distortions in policy.

The political balance in contests between the public and private interest is never determined simply by the democratic adding machine. Wealth has influence in the political process, whether exercised through donations to political parties, or spending to shape public opinion, or in other ways. The big question for this chapter is whether changes in the way private forces seek to influence policy has removed the possibility of governing in the public interest in the twenty-first century.

Politics in a democracy is inevitably a contest between groups seeking efficient policy for economic development and equity, and other groups seeking interventions to confer special benefits upon themselves or to kill or constrain interventions that would impose unwanted costs.

Private interests can misrepresent and campaign against a reform programme in ways that make choices in the public interest difficult and unlikely. They have powerful incentives to obscure the real effects of interventions. By contrast, those seeking greater economic efficiency and equity have an interest in independent analysis, transparency and public education.

Similarly, as noted in Chapter 3, private interests have a large advantage in the concentration of benefits from particular interventions on a small number of recipients. These beneficiaries know exactly who they are, and are prepared to invest a proportion of the gains from favourable interventions to secure their continuance. By contrast, those seeking to advance the public interest are handicapped by the free rider constraints on collective action. None of the many diffuse beneficiaries of any particular act of good policy will have a strong interest in seeking out reliable and comprehensive information on the effects of that policy and persuading others of its merit.

That explains why good policy for economic efficiency and equity is the exception rather than the rule. It explains Australia's chronic economic underperformance through most of its history, and the quick restoration after the Reform Era of approaches that are unlikely to sustain prosperity.

Political leaders and parties can associate themselves with public interest objectives, or align themselves with private interests. In the latter case, they can catch a ride on others' marketing of a deceitful version of the common good. These are ancient verities of political systems; the ride is simply faster with sophisticated modern channels of influence.

In the early twenty-first century we have seen a reversion to the old behaviour of interest groups from before the Reform Era, but we have also seen new ways of participating in the political process. One new development is the rise of partisan political campaigns from industry across a wide range of issues, whenever private interests are crossed by proposals for policy change. These have been conducted without the more or less sophisticated appeal to the public interest that would have been necessary for a hearing in the Reform Era. This adds to the difficulty of Australia's adjustment to the end of the China boom.

A NEW APPROACH TO GAINING INFLUENCE

The first large-scale campaign in the new style was that by the union movement against the Howard government's WorkChoices industrial relations policy. The trade unions spent about $30 million on the campaign. This intervention is credited with having been hugely influential in the 2007 general election that led to the formation of the Rudd Labor government. The most elaborate analysis of the campaign suggests it had a significant effect in twenty-five marginal seats that were the focus of intensive effort, although the Rudd government would have been elected without it. The reputation of its success has deterred the Coalition from considering any substantial change to industrial relations since that time.

This was no ordinary issue. It raised anxiety about working conditions in a large part of the population. It was therefore likely to be fertile ground for action by an effective opposition.

For business, the campaign against the Resources Super Profits Tax (RSPT) has become the model for action. This new tax on mining profits was one of many changes recommended by the Henry Taxation Review. The government announced mid-afternoon on Sunday,

2 May 2010 that this and a small number of other recommendations would be implemented.

The Henry Review's RSPT was put forward as a tax on mineral rent. If structured correctly, a rent tax can collect substantial revenue without deterring the development of new mines or the expansion of established ones. However, there were a number of problems with the review and its RSPT recommendations that made it especially vulnerable to attack.

While the secretary for the Treasury was eminently qualified to lead such work, he was also to advise the government on its policy response to the review's recommendations. This did not give the review or its response the necessary independence from government, which inevitably affected assessment of the recommendations.

While resource rent taxation was familiar to relevant parts of Australian business and independent analysts through the Petroleum Resource Rent Tax (PRRT), which had operated for over a quarter of a century, the RSPT was new to citizens and firms in Australia, and to the industry everywhere. This form of taxation was only ever understood by a few of the academic specialists and one or two media commentators who were called upon to play a role in the public discussion. It was not understood by the ministers who had to explain it to the electorate. Its unfamiliarity made it unsuitable for immediate implementation; at best, it required lengthy public discussion, analysis and assessment.

Unfamiliarity was not its only problem. If the RSPT had been tabled for public discussion with the Report of the Henry Review and subjected to critical analysis, there would have been widespread agreement on the need for substantial modification – in my view, in the direction of the PRRT. Successful implementation of the RSPT also required intensive communication and an eventual agreement with the states. There was no intensive communication, let alone agreement.

When the commonwealth budget for 2010–11 was unveiled later in May, it included revenue from the RSPT in the estimates, leaving no easy room for discussion with the industry. While it is unusual and bad practice to negotiate taxation parameters with affected taxpayers, it is normal and good practice to consult on how a new tax would work, with a view to incorporating knowledge uncovered during consultations in government's final decisions.

The mining industry, led by the two largest companies, reacted with unprecedented fury to the announcement of the new tax. The Minerals Council of Australia spent $17 million, and individual mining companies and a smaller association $5 million, on a six-week advertising campaign against the tax and the government. The campaign was stopped after factional Labor leaders secured the replacement of Kevin Rudd by Julia Gillard and the new government entered into negotiations with the three largest mining companies on the replacement of the RSPT.

Things got worse after the change of prime minister. Gillard supervised the negotiation of a hastily constructed alternative based on the structure of the PRRT. This new tax, the MRRT, was confined to iron ore, coal and petroleum.

Its initial flaws were compounded when a former chairman of BHP Billiton with apparent conflicts of interest was appointed to chair a committee to recommend on transitional arrangements. A commonwealth minister was a member of this committee – an anomalous position for someone who would be required to join the Cabinet to consider its recommendations.

The general form of the MRRT that emerged from this complex process was sound. However, it contained several problematic features that were never publicly explained or discussed before legislation. The transitional arrangements effectively exempted income from profitable established mines for many years, even if they had already recouped historical investments with high rates of return and continued to be highly profitable. Without good reason, the tax covered only part of the mining and petroleum industries. The rates of return allowed on investment were higher and the rates of taxation lower than for the established PRRT, which had operated with general comfort for a quarter of a century. And the relationship between the new commonwealth tax and state royalties was bound to be a source of economic distortion and instability.

The government accepted advice that the revised tax would still generate large amounts of revenue. These expectations were written into the budget. The eventual failure of the tax to yield the revenue contributed to the corrosion of the government's reputation for fiscal competence.

And yet – despite the RSPT coming out of an inappropriate process, being badly designed and appallingly implemented, and being subject to huge activist opposition from the mining industry – there was considerable support in the electorate for the original proposal.

Several polling groups measured attitudes to the RSPT through the six weeks of conflict. The questions asked were not identical, but a general picture emerges of slightly larger support than opposition on the tax's announcement. The proportion of supporters fell over the six weeks, to end up a bit smaller than opponents at the end. The responses were different in the one poll, late in the contest, on 23 May, in which respondents were told that the revenue was to be used for reducing company tax, assisting small business and increasing superannuation; supporters at 43 per cent exceeded the 36 per cent against. The proportion opposed was fairly stable over the six weeks: the shift was from support to uncommitted.

The more important result was that the standing of the government rose steadily through the six weeks. We have Newspoll results for the weekend of the announcement (with interviews too early to be influenced by the RSPT announcement) and at two-week intervals. The first, taken on 1–2 May, was the worst Newspoll ever for the government under Kevin Rudd, with the slump immediately following his decision to abandon an attempt to legislate for an ETS – 49:51 against. Two weeks later, the poll had evened up to 50:50. With the battle continuing, the next poll was 51:49 in the government's favour. The final poll, taken with Rudd as prime minister but released on the day of his replacement, was 52:48 in favour of the government. Every poll has a margin of error and there are many other issues in play, but this series of observations demonstrates at least that the campaign by the mining companies did not damage the electoral standing of the government over this period.

Contrary to the conventional wisdom on the electoral politics of the RSPT, Rudd and the government won the contest in the electorate. The government failed on the issue because the process of policy development led to an unsatisfactory choice of taxation instrument, and then the leading figures in the Labor Party lost their nerve, failed to think through the consequences of toppling a prime minister under the circumstances of mid-2010, and let other agendas get in the way of the implementation of a contested policy. It was a failure within the Labor Party and the government, rather than a case of the power of mining companies exceeding that of a democratically elected government.

The episode is remembered as a caution to governments proposing policy that is opposed by large corporations. A clear-headed assessment suggests a different conclusion: that under the right conditions, a government acting in the public interest has considerable autonomy in standing up to the most powerful private interests *even when* they have committed large resources to the exercise of political influence. The right conditions include a wide public understanding of the issues, and coherence in the decision-making processes of the government.

Who was to blame for the fiasco? Companies can be expected to promote their own interests, whether or not these coincide with the public interest. Governments can be expected to defend the public interest. It is a pity for our democracy and for policy based on the public interest that this new approach by private interests to influencing policy entered Australia, but the failure to respond to it firmly in the public interest was unambiguously a failure of government. The Labor government did not hold firm in defence of the public interest.

The RSPT outcome is discussed internationally as a case of the subversion of democratic processes by corporate power. The change of prime minister and abandonment of the RSPT have been raised with me by wise and thoughtful Chinese who hope for a democratic future for their country. They have interpreted the dispute as a case of corporations having the power to overthrow a democratically elected prime minister within established Western models of democracy. A democracy in which that can happen, they say, is unattractive.

Chinese with other political inclinations have taken comfort from the power of money (of which they have plenty) to influence policy in a Western democracy. I have tried to explain to both groups that the affair was the failure of a government and not a failure of the democratic system.

There is an inclination for Chinese observers to accept what they are told by Western businesspeople about the power of money in our democracy. One top Chinese business leader with mining interests in Australia told me in 2011 that a leading Australian mining figure had advised him that there was no need to worry about the mining and carbon taxes: the miner had paid $2 million to Australian political parties to ensure that these taxes would be abolished after the next election.

Chinese observers who hoped well for democracy, as well as those who took comfort from the power of money in Australian politics, would both have taken a close interest in the 2013 election, when an Australian mining magnate decided to do away with the political middleman and secure his own representation in the Australian Parliament. The Palmer United Party went on to win three Senate seats. Clive Palmer, to his credit, has recognised the potential for conflict of interest. How this conflict is managed is a crucial matter for the reality and the perception of the integrity of Australian democracy.

For all its flaws, the MRRT that was legislated through this fiasco is now yielding some revenue. It will yield much more in any future years of exceptionally high commodity prices, in all the years that follow a large and durable currency depreciation, and after the exhaustion of the 'market value' transitional deductions in the 2020s. Removing the MRRT will have virtually no effect on mining companies' decisions regarding new investments, so it will not increase economic growth. The only practical economic effect of removing the MRRT will be to make the long-term budget challenge harder.

The RSPT conflict has inspired political campaigns to change policy by a large number of interest groups. It was followed by campaigns or threats of campaigns along similar lines by the gambling industry to block reform to restrict access to people with gambling problems; by the automotive-leasing industry to block reform of the fringe-benefits tax; by the pharmaceutical retailers to block reform of prescription drug supply; and by the tobacco industry to block plain packaging. The Opposition promised to give the corporate lobbyists the outcome that they sought on most issues. This helped to entrench the new political culture for the time being. It will be a rod for the back of the government, the breaking of which will require strong leadership from the prime minister, with support from the independent centre of the polity.

MINING-TAX POLITICS WAS ONCE DIFFERENT

To understand the extent of the change in political culture involved in the campaign against the RSPT, it is instructive to go back to the end of the Japan resources boom: the lift in minerals and energy prices of the early 1970s following the first oil shock of 1973. Global coal and oil prices rose several-fold in 1973 and 1974.

Australia's large coal exports, then mainly metallurgical coal from Queensland, were immediately subject to greatly increased rail freights by the monopoly Queensland railways, and an export tax by the commonwealth government. Australian crude oil, then mainly from Bass Strait, was entirely sold at fixed prices into the domestic market under a scheme established by the Menzies government in 1965 and modified by the Gorton government in 1970. The Fraser government allowed prices to rise to international levels in 1976, but imposed a crude-oil levy that absorbed for the commonwealth government virtually all of the increase in revenue from the higher price (amounting to 71 per cent of gross sales revenue in 2012–13, in addition to a royalty of 12.5 per cent still applying).

By the Fraser government's last full financial year in office, the levy (ignoring the old royalty) contributed about 1.9 per cent of GDP to revenue. If the same marginal rate of taxation had been applied to the increased revenue from higher coal and iron ore prices from established iron ore and coal mines in the China resources boom from 2003, these two parts of the mining industry on a conservative estimate would have contributed an additional $21 billion in revenue in 2012–13 after taking into account reduced corporate income-tax receipts. The 2012–13 budget would have seen a surplus rather than a deficit of $19 billion.

I do not draw on this history to commend the actions of Australian governments in the 1970s. Far from it. I was the most persistent critic of the Whitlam and Fraser governments' approaches to taxing mineral rents. A series of my papers with Anthony Clunies Ross was influential in the eventual replacement of the crude-oil levy by the PRRT. The Hawke government removed the crude-oil allocation system on my advice during the prime minister's first term. Free export prices and the PRRT generated large amounts of revenue – less than the crude-oil levy in the short term, but more in the long term due to the more efficient development of the petroleum sector.

I draw on this history only to demonstrate the huge change in political culture. The main company managing relations with government in both oil and coal was BHP. Then a mainly Australian-owned and Australian-managed company, it ran relations with government for its foreign 50:50 joint venture partner in Bass Strait. BHP and the smaller Australian companies affected by the policy changes grumbled but accepted the decisions of the democratically elected government. BHP's partners did not grumble publicly. The changes made by the government were seen as the sovereign right of governments and not as sovereign risk.

The PRRT is now seen as having made a substantial contribution to revenue, with minimal distortion of production and distribution decisions. Nevertheless, it was greeted critically by the Coalition Opposition of the day. 'Nothing could better illustrate the counter-productive nature of the Hawke government's energy policies,' said the shadow treasurer, John Howard. 'The Hawke government's RRT will effectively destroy the incentive for offshore exploration …'

As it turned out, offshore oil and gas exploration, development and production all expanded enormously. Prime Minister John Howard thought that the PRRT worked just fine – fine enough to leave it in place and generating substantial revenue for eleven years. If the new Abbott government were to retain the MRRT, it may be disappointed with the revenue yield for quite a while, but would find that the tax generated worthwhile amounts of revenue later on.

Like Howard before him, Prime Minister Abbott might come to think that the MRRT did no harm and generated an increasing amount of useful revenue. It would be helpful in meeting Australia's challenge in the years ahead if, after a respectful pause from the heat of recent opposition, the current government or its successor reassessed the limited coverage of the MRRT, as well as its anomalous differences with the PRRT. This should be done in the context of the new federal compact on financial relations discussed in Chapter 8. Otherwise we will have to start again on resources taxation within the reform of federal financial relations.

CARBON PRICING: A GOAL AGAINST THE RUN OF PLAY

The contest over climate change policy is more complex. This has been a big issue in the last three federal elections and, separately, in the last four changes of leadership in the major political parties. It will play a central role in the longevity of the Abbott government. The policies with an ETS at their centre that were legislated in 2011 and described in Chapter 9 are working as they were designed to do. This experience has eased anxieties that they would be economically disruptive. They have majority support in the electorate if viewed as a package, and there is stronger support for meeting emissions reduction targets than for the removal of the ETS. Nevertheless, the new government is committed to repealing the ETS.

Until July 2014, the government will not have a majority in the Senate by which to repeal the legislation. After then, repeal depends on the votes of a number of senators who are not aligned with either major party. The repeal has been described by the prime minister as part of his mandate to govern. If it is blocked in the Senate, the prime minister has said that he will dissolve both Houses of Parliament and call a general election to resolve the deadlock. The polling says that only a minority of the electorate supports a double dissolution of the Parliament – while a substantial majority stands by its election choice of prime minister.

I am not going to tell this richly textured and continuing story. It will take enough time and words to make a few observations about the role of private interests in the wider political story of climate change, and discuss how they interacted with other forces to influence policy and shape the perceptions of the electorate.

Australia has the highest emissions per person of the developed economies. Our exports contain an unusually high proportion of fossil fuels. Australian industry therefore contains a higher proportion of wealth generated from emissions-intensive industries than that of any other developed country except Norway. (Norway is different, because a major share of economic rents are generated within a state-owned corporation that does not play a private role in the political process.)

Australia also has unusually rich opportunities for developing low-emissions energy, but the established industries are currently small. The main developments will occur in the future, and the corporate and personal beneficiaries do not yet know that they stand to gain.

For the export industries, other countries' policies are more important than Australia's own. The Chinese and US discouragement of coal-based power generation has, in different ways, reduced the expected profitability of

Australian coal more than any action taken here to reduce its use.

It is inherent in the human condition that where most people stand on an issue depends at least to an extent on where they sit. Many senior Australian businesspeople have a vested interest in the failure of global efforts to mitigate the dangers of climate change. One consequence is that our business leadership contains an unusually high proportion of people who express the opinion that the best of climate science is wrong on global warming.

There are exceptions. The implications of climate change are so large that they challenge deep allegiances in the minds of intelligent people. The chief executive of one of the world's largest exporters of coal, with whom I discussed my work on climate change at length, shared with me the discomfort that he felt about the implications of coal use for the future human condition. He took comfort, he said, from the possibility that expanding coal use might be reconciled with climate stability by the successful capture and storage of carbon dioxide wastes. He was personally troubled by what he saw as the increasing probability that work on carbon capture and storage would not be successful, so that it may become necessary to acknowledge a contradiction.

It is more common for business leaders with interests in the fossil fuel industries to find other justifications for resisting policies to reduce emissions. Something should be done, they say, but now is not a good time. Or there is no point in Australia doing things before others. Yes, others are doing things, but they are not doing the same things that are being proposed for Australia. We should do something, but what is now being proposed is not achieving its objectives, or is unfair to my industry.

The most common and important initial stance of the major emitting industries in the Australian debate was to insist on more compensation for their activities. This went well beyond any economic justification. While the demands for greater compensation did not amount to direct opposition to the policies, acquiescence to them would have made the package as a whole irresponsible from the perspective of budget stability, or favoured corporate interests over ordinary households. This made these industries opponents in practice, if not in principle, of effective policies.

The business lobbies, including the Business Council of Australia, tended to relay the views of their most concerned members. Something should be done, they said, but what was being proposed contained 'flaws' that required its rejection. The fact that, by the criteria applied by the lobbies, all alternative policies had greater flaws was of no account.

Some business interests also participated in the political process by providing funds to organisations campaigning against climate science or mitigation policies. This usually reflected the strong personal views of particular people.

The most important role of private interests in practical policymaking on climate change was to weaken support for any particular measure. Something should be done in general to mitigate climate change, but nothing in particular. The private interests contributed to the political smog through which policymakers had to find their way.

Leaders of large firms and the business lobbies remained silent when the Opposition, now the government, committed itself to replacing carbon pricing with an interventionist approach to mitigation that will make it much more expensive and disruptive for Australia to meet its international commitments.

As with the RSPT, the popular memory of the carbon-pricing package, promoted by the majority of the print media, is that it has been highly unpopular. 'The hated carbon tax' became a stock phrase in the News Corp majority press and on page two of the *Australian Financial Review*.

The reality is more complex. Despite the smog blown out by Australian business and its lobbies, the systematic distortion of the issues in the majority News Corp press, the relentless criticism from the Opposition since its change of leadership in December 2009, and the absence of advocacy of legislated policies from the Labor government, there has been continued public support for action on climate change in general – *and* for the 2011 measures when viewed as a package. That support has been stronger when comparisons are made with any alternative policies.

Attitudes to the policy depend on whether people think climate change is real; if real, whether they think it is caused by humans; and if caused by humans, whether they think that the policy represents a good response.

Newspoll provides consistent findings. Australians have overwhelmingly considered climate change to be real: 84 per cent in July 2008, falling to a low of 73 per cent in February 2011 soon after the change of Opposition leadership, and rising gradually from there. Nearly all who considered climate change real thought that humans were wholly or partly responsible, at the beginning and at the end. A majority supported a price on carbon to slow it down, even at the cost of higher petrol, electricity and gas prices (57 per cent in December 2010, 54 per cent in May 2011).

Australians expressed overwhelming support for the Rudd government's Carbon Pollution Reduction Scheme (CPRS) when it was also supported by the federal Opposition (72 per cent in October 2008, 67 per cent in September 2009), and merely strong support after the change in Opposition leadership and policy (57 per cent in February 2010).

Bitterly attacked from the beginning as a 'great big new tax' that would put a wrecking ball through the economy, the legislated carbon price had much less support than the CPRS in May 2011 (30 per cent support; 60 per cent opposition). In fact, the 2011 package was similar to the CPRS, with two departures that registered with the community – the increase in the tax-free threshold funded by the carbon pricing, which was popular; and the higher fixed price for a three-year transition period, which was unpopular when the 2010 decline in the European price left it high by international standards. The most important of the other differences provided for better governance of the 2011 scheme, which did not attract community interest.

Most polls did not ask about the package as a whole, as distinct from the 'carbon tax' component. When polls asked respondents what they thought about carbon pricing when the whole of the revenue was going to be used for tax cuts, household social security payments, renewable energy and compensation for industry – as it was in the 2011 package – the package received consistent majority support. For some reason, which may have had its origins in the focus group, the government mostly chose not to present the carbon pricing and household payments as a single package. If the separation was to allow the government to receive separate recognition for the cut in income tax (principally by raising the tax-free threshold), it backfired politically. The Opposition also separated the carbon pricing from the tax cut and household payments, and then promised the good bits without the bad, at a large cost to the budget.

While there was a strongly negative view of carbon pricing in isolation, the polls reveal majority opposition to repealing it, majority opposition to a double dissolution election on the issue and, before the election, support for the carbon pricing policy on its own over the Coalition's proposal for Direct Action.

These views were clearly observed even among Coalition voters in an exit poll at the 2013 election conducted by JWS Research and commissioned by the Climate Institute. Reminded that the Coalition supported targets of reducing emissions unconditionally by 5 per cent and conditionally by up to 25 per cent, 40 per cent of Coalition voters thought it more important to meet the targets than to repeal the carbon 'tax', and only 32 per cent that it was more important to repeal the tax. Only 3 per cent thought that 'scrapping the carbon tax' was the most important of the issues that the Coalition had put to voters.

An Essential Vision Poll on 1 October 2013 provides insights into changes in opinion with the new government in place. Respondents were asked whether they supported 'the previous Labor Government's carbon pricing scheme which requires industry to pay a tax on the amount of carbon pollution they emit' (no mention was made of how the revenue would be used). Whereas the responses were evenly balanced in May 2013 (43:43), there were more negative responses after the election (39:37). Asked directly whether they preferred the carbon tax (no mention of the use of the revenue), or the Liberal Party's policy on providing funds for planting trees and paying companies to reduce carbon emissions, a majority supported the 'carbon tax' in May (39:29), but a minority after the election (31:35).

The smog of politics encouraged by private interests increased the difficulty of introducing a carbon-pricing package, and provided cover for a relentless attack on its central feature, but it did not turn majority opinion against the package as a whole. With firm and agile prime ministerial leadership, the Gillard government was able to legislate an effective policy. This time, in contrast to what happened with the mining tax, the government (and the Parliament) held its ground against huge pressure from private interests.

The main long-term consequence of the smog may turn out to be the cover it provided for the survival of an economically and environmentally weak alternative that can be expected to have disappointing results.

The Abbott Opposition was effective in its attacks on the 'great big new tax' because of two things that will not be part of future debates. One was Prime Minister Gillard's acquiescence to the leader of the Opposition's description of an ETS with an initially fixed price as a 'tax'. This could then be presented as a breach of the commitment that there would be no carbon tax under a government that she led. The second was the gap that opened up between the level of the fixed price in the first three years of the scheme ($23 and rising) when European carbon prices, initially well above that level, fell to around $A5 ($A7–8 in September 2013) as economic activity foundered and the European target became much less costly to achieve. The linking of the Australian ETS to Europe meant that this price discrepancy would have been removed from July 2015. Prime Minister Rudd, in July 2013, said that the link to Europe would be brought forward to July 2014 if he won the 2013 election.

Any regulation to reduce emissions involves costs that are as real as, and larger per unit of carbon emissions than, carbon pricing. The sum of the costs of mitigation measures – mostly Direct Action, not carbon pricing – in 2013 in Europe, the United States or China (as a proportion of household income or of the economy) is much higher than the costs to households or business of the $A23 fixed price in Australia once the distribution of the permit sales revenue is taken into account.

This is too complicated a point to be widely understood under the smog of attack by private interests and the Opposition. As a consequence, it is politically impracticable to maintain a carbon price that is higher than in Europe in these circumstances. The linking of the Australian scheme to Europe recognises this reality. It follows that carbon pricing here, as elsewhere, must be supplemented for longer than originally anticipated by other regulatory interventions if we are to achieve cuts that are commensurate with those in other countries.

While we do not yet know the relevant details of how Direct Action would work, analysis of the information available indicates that it would be more costly for

Australia to meet our targets through Direct Action than through an ETS linked to Europe. So the repeal of the 2011 legislation would mean that the smog had obscured the victory of private interests over the living standards of Australians. Or, if the high costs of Direct Action deter a serious effort to meet our commitments to the international community, it will have obscured the victory of private interests over the international effort to reduce the dangers of climate change.

Does this suggest that it is now impossible to implement policy in the public interest in Australia? Let's not rush to judgment. The smog did not prevent the legislation and implementation of a strong policy package. Indeed, the 2011 legislation stands out as a goal for market-oriented reform scored against the run of play in the mature years of the Great Australian Complacency. With the disparate objectives of minority senators, one cannot be certain yet that the package will not survive the Senate's consideration of repeal bills. And if repeal succeeds, it was a sufficiently close-run thing for other outcomes to have been possible.

CONFLICTS OF INTEREST ARE INCREASING

Most holders of high office and their close advisers through most of our democratic history have sought their reward in the satisfaction of performing well a role that is important to the community. In the apt words of Tony

Abbott on taking office, a life in high policy is a vocation. It is an honour to serve the people of your country in a way that improves their lives.

Some people close to the exercise of power have always had other motives. Some have seen the attainment of high office or influence as a largely commercial activity – a way to a more lucrative career and a path to wealth. We have succeeded as a nation because few of our most senior leaders have involved themselves in politics and policy with pecuniary motives. For example, our three long-serving post-war Coalition prime ministers, Menzies, Fraser and Howard, have been exemplary in their living of their vocations.

The revelation of corruption in the NSW state government's administration of mineral leases has shocked us. Yet this terrible case is in a sense reassuring, because the crimes will attract an appropriate punishment.

Less blatant but nonetheless seriously damaging uses of official office for the advancement of business interests are now accepted as normal. It is now normal for people to move directly and without delay from senior government roles into positions in which their intimate knowledge of personnel and processes has high commercial value. It is now normal for people to move directly from positions of confidential influence in the offices of heads of government and ministers into lobbying roles for companies in which their access to decision-makers and presumed influence over them is a valuable asset.

Do we really think it is right for a minister of the Crown with a portfolio related to gambling, who is also a recent state secretary of the governing party, to move directly to work for a company in the gambling business that has huge private interests in issues before the federal and state governments? Or for federal and state ministers to move straight into lobbying businesses, or positions with investment banks, in which at least part of their value derives from their influence over decisions of relevance to their new employers?

The revolving door was an important factor in the political contests over resource taxation and carbon pricing. It is a serious counterweight to the public interest in shaping contemporary policy. As the influence of money grows, we need to defend the integrity of the democratic process with a sensitivity that may have seemed unnecessary in earlier generations. We have to be clear and straightforward in our management of conflict of interest and the use of public office to advance private pecuniary ends.

The Commonwealth Public Service has a well-earned reputation for integrity. To preserve that integrity, we must defend its best traditions when they are breached. It is unfortunate that strong and prompt action was not taken on two 21st-century revelations of corrupt behaviour in areas of commonwealth responsibility: the Australian Wheat Board's relationship with the regime of Saddam Hussein in Iraq; and the payment of bribes by the Reserve

Bank's note-printing subsidiaries. Justice was not seen to be done in relation to people who may have had responsibility in various ways for serious corruption.

The election of three Palmer United Party senators at the 2013 election requires us to think through how we manage conflict-of-interest issues in our Parliament. The leader of the party, Clive Palmer, has major mining interests, including in Queensland coal, that would be affected by the removal of carbon pricing. (They would also be affected by the removal of the MRRT; while quantitatively of less importance, the principle is the same.) Palmer has made it clear that the three senators will be subject to party discipline under his leadership in using their votes within the Senate.

Palmer has been asked whether he would withdraw from his mining investments if elected to the Parliament. He responded that he would handle the conflict in the way that would be appropriate on the board of a public company: by removing himself from discussions affecting his interests.

Palmer's expressed concern about the role of lobbyists in our political life is a positive and welcome contribution to a debate that should go much further. His statement that he would recuse himself from decisions affecting his own private interests is welcome and appropriate. It is important that the leader of the Palmer United Party advise senators who have acknowledged his leadership to adopt the same approach: they too should recuse themselves from decisions in which their leader has a material pecuniary interest. The democratic legitimacy of a Senate decision to abolish carbon pricing that depended on votes from the Palmer United Party would be tainted.

The early twenty-first century has seen a major change in the role of private interests in the policymaking process that has made reform in the public interest more difficult. This has placed a smog over the policymaking process, rather than an impenetrable wall. It has created an environment in which governments can lose their nerve and do the bidding of private interests. However, the evidence so far indicates that private interests are still not able to block a government with a clear idea of its objectives and which seeks to appeal to the electorate in the name of the public interest.

CONCLUSION

I am writing this in the week after the September 2013 election. The data that comes in week by week is confirming that the economy is growing well below capacity. Employment is growing much less rapidly than the working-age population. The resources industries are subtracting from growth in incomes. Our competitiveness in resources continues to decline as the exchange rates of all our main competitors fall much more than our own: Indonesia and South Africa for coal; Brazil (and sometimes India) for iron ore; Russia for natural gas and other minerals to China. There are no signs yet of an expansion in investment and production of the industries outside resources – nor should we expect this with Australian costs way above those of other countries.

The mood among business is a bit better than before the election, but the economic fundamentals are a bit worse. The exchange rate has retraced some of its decline. Estimates of the budget deficit for this and future years were greatly increased at the end of August 2013, and yet we are now much more comfortable with the bigger deficit than we were with a smaller one.

The election has been followed by a shift from talking down to talking up the economy in the News Corp majority press. Consumer and business confidence has continued to rise since the August cut in interest rates. There has been a lift in some of the financial markets. There is talk that increased confidence from the change of government will lift spending and economic activity, and even that the resources boom will burst back into life. That the employment and growth and budget and external payments challenges will go away.

Sorry. That's not the way the economy works. Increased investment in any industry is shaped by calculations of expected profit. None of the purported increase in confidence and none of the high-profile election promises of the government will change profit calculations in ways that increase investment. None will help us to meet the fundamental challenge: to improve Australian competitiveness and to increase investment and activity in trade-exposed industries while keeping the budget on a path to long-term stability.

There are some mercies. Unlike in the early months of 2013, no one close to the levers of power is saying anymore that a strong dollar is unavoidable and possibly desirable – but nor is anyone saying that there is an urgent need to improve Australian competitiveness. In fact, the government has said that it will not make any large policy change to lift productivity until after another election.

The public signs are that policy has settled into somewhere between the 'business as usual' and 'budget stimulus' approaches identified in Chapter 5. The treasurer has spoken of increasing infrastructure investment as a stimulus to the economy after the resources boom. Public spending on infrastructure is a good way to provide stimulus, and much better if it is guided by sound analysis of the costs and benefits of alternative investments. Somewhere between business as usual and stimulus is a better place to be than austerity, which had such prominent support from much of the political elite in the media, business and Opposition through the last Parliament. But it cannot be the main response to our challenge.

Business as usual plus stimulus may lift employment and output, as it did in the crisis following the Great Crash of 2008. But it won't do it sustainably, because our budget and external financial outlooks are weaker now. Stimulus is just storing up problems for the future unless there is a large real depreciation. And if there is a large real depreciation, not so much of a stimulus is needed to restore full employment.

The fall in the Australian dollar so far in 2013 helps, but it is not nearly enough. We may get lucky and the tightening of monetary policy in the United States and elsewhere may take the dollar lower again. Or it may not

– or not until the chance to avoid high unemployment is behind us.

As noted, the hard part of the adjustment will be turning the fall in the exchange rate into a real depreciation. Real depreciation means decreasing real incomes for many businesses and households, and for Australians on average. There are beneficiaries of real depreciation in the trade-exposed industries, notably farming. But these are much fewer than the average Australian who has to tighten her belt. The biggest beneficiaries are those people who would otherwise have lost their jobs or whose businesses would have been damaged or destroyed in a much bigger downturn. They will not even know their good fortune because they will be unaware of the fate that has been avoided.

The politics will be all about the many who must accept lower real incomes. That is politically difficult in any context. It does not happen at all without effective leadership and public education based on a sound programme of reform to improve efficiency and equity.

The fall in the dollar so far has occurred without a framework for turning it into a real depreciation. There will be resistance and political tension associated with every bit of the squeeze on living standards. Whether the policies can be maintained through this pressure will depend on whether the prime minister and his government can explain the necessity and the fairness of what is being done. In short, making this big adjustment work depends on building a new reform era.

The new Australian political culture makes a prime minister seeking to govern in the public interest vulnerable to attack from an Opposition focused on unpopular developments and measures. The Dog Days provide exceptional opportunities for negativity. The approach of the Opposition matters for reform. Whatever it might do to its own hopes for early return to government, an Opposition that offers broadly constructive support for a new reform era, with criticism focusing on departures from a clearly articulated conception of the public interest, would improve the prospects of a successful Australian transition.

AVOIDING THE NEED FOR SUCH PAIN IN THE FUTURE

Australians should be able to agree on one big lesson from this latest episode of resources boom and decline. When strong growth in newly industrialising countries increases demand for our commodities, neither government nor business knows how much of the increase is here to stay.

History tells us that after a period of boom, commodity prices usually pull back a long way. Because we do not know how much of the increase will stay with us, governments should hold back on spending most of the increment in revenue until we know more. The reason for this is that it is painful, politically difficult and economically wasteful to increase costs and force changes in industry to accommodate them, and then to remove the increases in living standards and costs and rebuild the industries that have been destroyed. Better to wait and see whether the changes are necessary at all.

A second reason for delaying the spending of revenue from high export prices is that they are likely to be followed by an investment boom to expand supply. This increases the demand for domestic labour and supplies, while pushing up domestic costs and the real exchange rate. Best not to let increased government spending exacerbate the increase in costs. If government has saved the increased revenue from the temporarily high export prices, it can spend it on infrastructure and in other productive ways when the boom is receding.

The lessons are similar for the private sector. Temporarily high prices are not a licence for reckless expansion. Caution will avoid the destruction of value that comes with writing down boom-time capital investments when the end of the boom makes production unprofitable. There is no need for a repetition of the destruction of shareholder wealth that we have seen in the Australian thermal coal industry in 2012 and 2013.

These are old lessons that we should not have had to learn anew. We had to learn them anew because many people thought that this time was different. They thought that this time was different because in the huge Chinese economy there was no limit to demand for the goods that Australia supplied. Above all, this time was different because the Reform Era had instilled a new flexibility in the Australian economy, so that if our costs and real exchange rate rose when prices and investment were temporarily high, they would fall smoothly, without cost and painlessly if and when the boom ended.

'This time' never turns out to be completely different. Never different enough to warrant the abandonment of prudence.

Would it help to save the increment of revenue in a sovereign fund, as Norwegians and others have done with success and profit? Yes, if it helps to institutionalise the idea that the higher revenues are temporary and should be saved. Yes, if it makes it easier politically not to spend the increased revenue. There is nothing magical about a sovereign wealth fund to manage cyclical variations in revenue, but if it helps with saving boom-time revenue, let's have it in place for the next time round.

HOW WILL YOU KNOW IF I AM WRONG?

I began the book by saying there are two possible futures for Australia in the period ahead. One is business as usual (now with talk of it being tempered by stimulus spending on infrastructure). This gives us economic growth well below our capacity of 3 and a bit per cent per annum, slowly deteriorating employment conditions for a growing population, and a slow squeeze on real incomes. The officially projected budget surplus in 2016–17 does not materialise. The modest economic growth is worse than it looks because it is dominated by increased resource exports that contribute relatively little to Australian jobs and incomes.

The other possible future contains an early and large real depreciation, with a hard start but better outcomes. A fair distribution of the burdens of adjustment, and strong reform to raise productivity and efficiency, are part of the 'real depreciation' strategy. Greater spending on demonstrably productive infrastructure is a useful complement to depreciation.

Other contributors to the contemporary Australian economic discussion say there are other alternatives. The resources boom will revive, and consumption and investment are about to take off. The reader will know soon enough who is right and who is wrong – but alas, not soon enough to avoid hard years for many Australians if my diagnosis is correct.

I have written with some confidence because I have been living for a long time with the issues raised in this book. But let us remember the story of Chapter 1. The big currents of economic development are inherently uncertain. China may fail in the implementation of its ambitious structural reform; this would hold up some of Australia's resources boom for a while and then dump us much harder. A combination of other large developing countries may grow so strongly that we enter a new resources boom in a few years' time. A new crisis in financial markets could appear as the developed countries' central banks phase out their exceptional monetary policies.

The policy reforms that I have suggested in Part 2 would give us a good start on doing harder things if the future deals us a worse hand than I have anticipated. And it will do no large harm to have started to improve competitiveness and avoided excessive expansion of domestic spending if the future unfolds in a favourable way.

You will know that I was unnecessarily worrying my fellow citizens if the weakening labour market of the past two years goes into reverse before too long and takes us back to the full employment of the official projections in 2015–16, and if the budget deficit starts shrinking rapidly after this year (as in the official projections) – and all without large real depreciation or concern about the financing of our external deficits.

However, the reader should be worried that I might be right if the availability of employment for a growing population continues to drift downwards and there are no signs of increased investment in trade-exposed industries. Or if we deal with immediate employment problems by increasing domestic spending without a big improvement in competitiveness, and Australian indebtedness to foreigners starts to grow strongly again.

I hope that neither of these latter circumstances arises. But if they do, we will have to make a late start on the largest adjustment challenge to face any but the oldest living Australians.

WHAT IF AUSTRALIA GETS IT WRONG?

If I am right and Australia gets it right, we will endure a period of moderate falls in living standards, without any part of our society suffering badly from the adjustment. After a while, living standards will start to rise again – moderately, in line with the higher productivity growth that a new reform era has made possible. We will be in a sound position to manage any major disruption to the international economy. We will feel comfortable with our democracy, and others will see our democratic capitalism in a positive light.

Tolstoy tells us in the opening of *Anna Karenina* that every happy family is the same, while each unhappy family is unhappy in its own way. He oversimplified the story of happy families, but he was right that there are many ways that things can go badly.

If we fail to take an early opportunity to adjust down the cost levels that have hung over from the China resources boom, we can look forward to economic instability, inflation, stagnation and high unemployment. Governments will do their best to deal with parts of the problem where solutions seem to be constrained less tightly by political reality, and stir up new nests of opposition for their troubles. We will become an unlucky country, run by second-rate people who share the country's bad luck.

The downside from getting it wrong is big. Rising and high unemployment and business failures would place great stress on many of our people and on our institutions.

If our country fails the challenge, Australians would be foolish to ignore the weakness in our democracy that contributed to failure – the rise in power of private interests; the fragmentation of the national conversation about policy; increasing comfort with conflict of interest. We would be wise to heed the lessons from the political history of other resource-rich countries in which democratic institutions have been broken by the power of resource-based wealth.

It matters to Australians that the public interest wins in the great struggle to shape the aftermath of the China resources boom. At a pivotal time in the spread of modern economic development throughout the world, the fate of democratic capitalism in our ancient continent matters for others as well.

ACKNOWLEDGMENTS

The central economic policy idea in this book is that the prospects of full employment and low inflation without external financing problems are determined jointly by the levels of expenditure and competitiveness, and not by the level of expenditure alone. The intellectual origins of this idea go back to James Meade (including his visit to Australia in the 1930s), Roland Wilson, Trevor Swan and then Max Corden. Failure to apply this insight was a cause of the Australian recessions of 1974–75, 1982–83 and 1990–91. Marx said, in his reflections on the rise of Louis Napoleon, that history repeats itself the first time as tragedy and then as farce. This books tries to help Australians to avoid having to find a word to contain both tragedy and farce.

On the macro-economic framework, I have benefited a great deal from discussions over recent years with Max Corden, Peter Jonson, David Gruen, Martin Parkinson, Gordon de Brouwer, David Vines and Glenn Stevens. Of course, none should be blamed for the resting place of my thoughts that is recorded in this book. I have received helpful comment on the evolving macro-economic issues from seminars and conferences at which I have discussed versions of the macro-economic framework at the University of Melbourne on several occasions (including a joint seminar with Peter Jonson at the Institute of Applied Economic and Social Research), the Australian Treasury, the Australian National University, the Economics Society of Australia (separately at the ACT and Victorian branches), Victoria University, Peking University and the Australian Agricultural and Resource Economics Society.

The book also has a micro-economic reform dimension. Interaction with colleagues at the University of Melbourne is responsible for much that is of value in my suggestions in this area. The work led by Deborah Cobb-Clark at the Melbourne Institute and of Sue Richardson in Adelaide has helped to shape perspectives on the labour market and income distribution. The work of colleagues at the Melbourne Institute of Applied Economic Research and the seminar at the new Mitchell Institute at the University of Victoria was particularly helpful for the chapter on effectiveness of government. My colleague John Freebairn at Melbourne has sharpened up my thoughts on business taxation reform and has more important things to say himself, and Tom Abhayaratna helped with insights from the Henry Review and other work on tax reform.

The thoughts on resources taxation go back to my joint work with Anthony Clunies Ross in the 1970s and early 1980s. The discussion of the Australian Federation owes much to my joint work with Vince FitzGerald more than a decade ago. (Incidentally, in noting with thanks Bob Hawke's careful reading of the draft manuscript, I should register that Bob disagrees with my generally positive view of the potential value of the Federation.) The ideas about the context of Asian and Chinese economic growth have come from my longstanding collaboration with colleagues in the Crawford School of Economics and Governance at the Australian National University. The thoughts on climate change come out of work with the excellent Garnaut Climate Change Review secretariats led by Ron Ben-David in 2007–08 and Steven Kennedy in 2010–11, and my continuing interaction with those teams and people working in this field at the University of Melbourne, the Australian National University, the University of Queensland, the Grattan Institute and the Climate Institute.

The book is also about the political culture and political economy of reform. I was privileged to work closely with those who were responsible for Australia's great Reform Era from 1983 to the end of the century. Thanks especially to Graham Evans for comments on the draft manuscript from the experience of those times.

Thanks for help beyond the call of friendship and collegiality to Max Corden. Max's many careful readings of and commentary on drafts helped me to identify and clarify opaque presentation and argument. Any errors of logic that remain are, of course, entirely mine. Thanks too to my University of Melbourne colleagues Glyn Davis and Maxine McKew for helpful comments on draft chapters.

Thanks to my publishers Black Inc. and especially Chris Feik for excellent editorial advice and support and also enjoyable interaction in the challenging task of turning an economist's tendency to argue points at unconscionable length into a book that I hope can be read by a wide range of people who care about the future of our country; and to Anna Lensky for her work on introducing the book to people for whom it should be of interest.

Thanks as always to Veronica Webster, who contributed excellent support for research on many matters and work of great reliability on the endnotes and references.

Special thanks to Jayne and John Garnaut for much discussion of the subject of the book and for comments on drafts.

Ross Garnaut
University of Melbourne
1 October 2013

NOTES

1   'There are Salad Days': An edited version of this talk to the Economics Society was published in the *Oxford Review of Economic Policy* (Garnaut 2005a). So far as I know, William Shakespeare introduced the expression 'Salad Days' into our language through the voice of Cleopatra reflecting on her youthful dalliance with Julius Caesar: 'My salad days, when I was green in judgement, cold in blood …' *Antony and Cleopatra*, Act 1, Scene 5. The term 'Dog Days' is of Ancient Roman and, before that, Greek and Egyptian lineage. It originally referred to the hottest days of the Mediterranean midsummer, when tempers frayed; when the dog star Sirius appears in the early morning sky just at or before sunrise.

5   'the longest unbroken period of economic expansion': These comparisons are drawn from national accounts data converted into a common international currency at contemporary exchange rates.

11   'more damaging than … in 1990–91': See my presentations to the CLSA China Forum 2013 on 14 May 2013, and to the 'Monetary Policy and the Exchange Rate for the End of the Resources Boom: Two Different Views' seminar at the University of Melbourne on 24 May 2013 and the Treasury in Canberra on 7 June 2013, all available at www.rossgarnaut.com.au.

18   'capitalism works because': Hirsch 1976.

22   'Modern economic growth originated': I covered this ground in my

address to the 2012 Annual Meeting of the Consortium of Humanities Centres and Institutes, 'Can Humanity Manage the Anthropocene: The Challenge of Climate Change' (Garnaut 2012).

23 'contributed by population growth': Maddison 2001. See also Garnaut 2013a.

26 'growth rates around 3–4 per cent': Data about growth rates here and elsewhere in the book are taken from the World Bank, World Development Report, various years.

28 'productivity growth slumped': Gordon 2012.

30 'the increased influence of money': Sachs 2012; Krugman 2007; Stiglitz 2012.

31 'affected much less by the Great Crash': Garnaut with Llewellyn-Smith 2009.

31 'This development falls into three periods': For more detail see Garnaut, Cai and Song 2013.

37 'The averages hide some important details': Leigh 2013.

38 'yearned to be free': See Marsh 1995 and Kelly 1992.

39 'all contributed to stagnation': Shann 1927.

40 'in response to foreign exchange shortages': Schedvin 1989.

42 'Australia's terms of trade rose': McLean 2013.

42 'a global slump': Garnaut 1979.

45 'winding back of protection': Rattigan 1986; Garnaut 1994a; Anderson and Garnaut 1987; Rattigan and Carmichael 1996.

46 'Independent reports': Campbell 1981; Martin 1991; Garnaut 1989; Hilmer 1993.

46 'multilateral trade negotiations for the first time': Garnaut 1994b, 1996 and 2005b; Elek 2009; Drysdale 1988; Drysdale and Garnaut 1993.

48 'three contrasting parts': Here and elsewhere, Australian economic data

are from Australian Bureau of Statistics sources, but assessed conveniently through the Reserve Bank of Australia's Statistical Tables.

50 'relinquished political control of monetary policy': MacFarlane 1996.

53 'Privatisation was preceded by careful work': See Evans 1992 and 1995 for an account of the work on regulation prior to privatisation in telecommunications and transport.

55 'A mostly helpful myth': The bit that was not myth was the strong support for market-oriented reform from part of the Liberal Party's representation in the Parliament through the 1980s and early 1990s. See Hyde 2002; Hewson and Fischer 1991.

56 'The quality of political leadership': There are many accounts of this period, none yet comprehensive in its coverage. Although his book project did not have the cooperation of Bob Hawke, Paul Kelly's *The End of Certainty: Power, Politics and Business in Australia* (1992) provides much relevant detail.

60 'I said to the Australia Unlimited Conference': This 1999 speech was published as Chapter 14 in Garnaut 2001. See Howard, 1999a, 1999b, 1999c, 1999d. My various other papers referred to in this chapter are available on my website, www.rossgarnaut.com.au, under the 'Australian Economy' tab.

69 'a meeting of a Senate Committee': Economics References Committee 2005.

87 'the increase was remarkable': Budget data are taken from the Australian Treasury, materials available on www.treasury.gov.au.

90 'September 2013 projections': The Bureau of Resources and Energy Economics 2013.

96 'the economic analysis underlying the policy choices': But for those who want to know more, the standard international macro-economic analysis

underlying this note and the book has its origins in Meade's 1951 classic *The Balance of Payments*. This was presented, in the form in which it has come to be known by most economists, by Trevor Swan (the Swan Diagram). Max Corden (2009) has made creative use of this approach in many articles, most recently in 'China's Exchange Rate Policy, Its Current Account Surplus, and the Global Imbalances'. Applications of standard international macro-economic analysis with floating currencies can be traced back to Mundell and Fleming. For a classic application of the analysis, see Max Corden's 1977 book, *Inflation, Exchange Rates and the World Economy: Lectures on International Monetary Economics*. For a more detailed application to the contemporary Australian situation, see Garnaut 2013b.

108 'beginning to bite': Commonwealth of Australia 2010.

109 'the fabled "Dutch Disease"': There is a considerable literature related to the Dutch Disease. The Australian literature began with Bob Gregory's 1976 paper 'Some Implications of the Growth of the Mineral Sector' in the *Australian Journal of Agricultural Economics*. See also Snape 1977; Corden and Neary 1982; Corden 2012.

121 'in his General Theory': Keynes 1936; Commonwealth of Australia 1945.

127 'uniquely well placed': For a detailed discussion of the implications of opportunities for Australia from growth in Asia in the early decades of the twenty-first century, see Commonwealth of Australia 2012.

130 'productivity isn't everything': Krugman 1994.

133 'excellent public institutions': The main data presented in this chapter are from the Australian Bureau of Statistics via the Productivity Commission's *2013 PC Productivity Update*, www.pc.gov.au/research/productivity/update/2013.

140 'Recent studies': The independent centre of the Australian polity has been

more active recently in discussing opportunities for increasing productivity. Various publications and public presentations from the Productivity Commission, the Grattan Institute and the Committee for the Economic Development of Australia are important. Note in particular Gary Banks's 2012 speech 'Productivity Policies: The "To Do" List'; Tony Wood's recent paper for the Grattan Institute (Wood et al. 2012); and CEDA's 2013 *Setting Public Policy* report. From Australian academia, I have found of particular value the paper by John Freebairn and Max Corden on investment in infrastructure as a stimulus measure (Freebairn and Corden 2013). For discussion of the costs of monopoly and the opportunities for reform see Craig Emerson's 2009 speech 'Labor Is the Party of Competition'. See also Garnaut 2013c.

141 'reform in one industry': Emerson 2009.

141 'monopoly power': A recent Parliamentary Committee reviewed and reported on the phenomenon of exceptionally high prices in Australia for internationally traded information technology products. See Standing Committee on Infrastructure and Communications 2013.

142 'comprehensive economy-wide reform': Garnaut 2011b; Wood et al. 2012; Productivity Commission 2013.

143 'Gas is a special problem': For an early authoritative assessment see Massachusetts Institute of Technology 2011.

151 'results of past work': Asprey 1975; Commonwealth of Australia 2012.

152 'Adam Smith advised': Smith 1776.

154 'seen to be fair': Our understanding of relationships between labour supply, household income, and health and education services is much richer now than ever before, to a significant extent because of the work at the University of Melbourne based on the HILDA model, and related surveys and analysis.

162 'now a small minority': Richardson 2013.

166 'the McClure Review': Reference Group on Welfare Reform 2000.

167 'in his book *Battlelines*': Abbott 2009.

169 'long-term opportunities': Vince FitzGerald and I set out proposals for reform in some detail in our 2002 *Review of Commonwealth-State Funding Final Report: A Review of the Allocation of Commonwealth Grants to the States and Territories*. Since then my thoughts have moved towards requiring a more complete separation of federal and state responsibilities than we suggested in 2002. See also the *2012 GST Distribution Review* by John Brumby, Bruce Carter and Nick Greiner, available online at www.gstdistributionreview.gov.au.

172 'have become joint responsibilities': I was helped in my thinking about these matters by a 2013 seminar at the Mitchell Institute for Health and Education Policy at Victoria University, which has been established to undertake research on health and education policy.

192 'a new component to climate change': An introduction to the voluminous literature on these matters can be found in the references cited in Garnaut 2008 and 2011a (both available online at www.garnautreview.org.au). For a recent update on the science, see the Intergovernmental Panel on Climate Change 2013, *Climate Change 2013: The Physical Science Basis* (www.ipcc.ch).

213 'History had ended': Fukuyama 1992 and 2012.

220 'an unrepresentative subset of reality': A careful study of reporting on climate change in the media has identified bias in reporting of the science in the three English-speaking countries in which News Ltd plays a major role, with Australia, the country in which the News Ltd role has been largest, standing out for the degree of bias. See Painter 2011.

223 'identified by Cicero': See Cicero and Carville 2012. I am grateful to

Nicholas Reece for drawing my attention to this classical insight into contemporary democratic practice.

227 'As Machiavelli explained': Machiavelli 1532.

236 'The most elaborate analysis': Spies-Butcher and Wilson 2008.

245 'the levy … contributed': The Fraser government's crude-oil levy in 1981–82 absorbed 72 per cent of the gross value of sales which, after the 12.5 per cent royalty, represented almost the whole of the increase in revenue from oil fields that were producing in 1976. The crude-oil levy only applied to 'old oil', and not to fields brought into operation after the introduction of the crude-oil levy. It included any increase in production from old fields. In the estimates of what a similar approach to the increase in iron ore and coal prices from 2002 would have yielded today, I have applied the crude-oil levy tax rates only to the volume of production in 2002. There has been considerable growth in output from established coal and iron ore mines since then.

247 'will effectively destroy': John Howard, 1 July 1984.

REFERENCES

Abbott, T., 2009, *Battlelines*, Melbourne University Press, Melbourne.

Anderson, K. and Garnaut, R., 1987, *Australian Protectionism: Extent, Causes and Effects*, Allen & Unwin, Sydney.

Asprey, K.W., *Taxation Review Committee Full Report,* 31 January 1975, Australian Government Publishing Service, Canberra.

Banks, G., 'Productivity Policies: The "To Do" List', Speech to the Economic and Social Outlook Conference, 'Securing the Future', Melbourne, 1 November 2012 <www.pc.gov.au/speeches/gary-banks/reform-agenda>.

Brumby, J., Carter, B. and Greiner, N., 2012, *GST Distribution Review,* Department of the Treasury, Canberra <www.gstdistributionreview.gov.au>.

The Bureau of Resources and Energy Economics, *Resources and Energy Quarterly*, September 2013 <www.bree.gov.au/documents/publications/req/REQ-2013-09.pdf>.

Campbell, J.K., 1981, *Australian Financial System: Final Report of the Committee of Inquiry into the Australian Financial System*, Australian Government Publishing Service, Canberra.

Cicero, Q.T. and Carville, J., 'Campaign Tips from Cicero: The Art of Politics, from the Tiber to the Potomac', *Foreign Affairs*, May/June 2012 <www.foreignaffairs.com/articles/137527/quintus-tullius-cicero-and-james-carville/campaign-tips-from-cicero>.

Committee of Economic Development of Australia, *Setting Public Policy*, August 2013 <www.ceda.com.au/research-and-policy/research/2013/08/setting-public-policy>.

Commonwealth of Australia, 1945, *Full Employment in Australia*, Australian Government Printer, Canberra.

Commonwealth of Australia, 2010, *Australia to 2050: Future Challenges (Intergenerational Report 2010)*, CanPrint Communications Pty Ltd, Canberra <archive.treasury.gov.au/igr>.

Commonwealth of Australia, *Australia in the Asian Century*, White Paper October 2012 <asiancentury.dpmc.gov.au>.

Corden, W.M., 1977, *Inflation, Exchange Rates and the World Economy: Lectures on International Monetary Economics*, Clarendon Press, Oxford.

Corden, W.M., 2009, 'China's Exchange Rate Policy, Its Current Account Surplus, and the Global Imbalances', *The Economic Journal*, Vol. 119, No. 541, pp. F430–F441.

Corden, W.M., 2012, 'The Dutch Disease in Australia: Policy Options for a Three-Speed Economy', *Melbourne Institute Working Paper No. 5/12*, the University of Melbourne <www.melbourneinstitute.com/miaesr/publications/working-paper-series/wps2012.html>.

Corden, W.M. and Neary, J.P., 1982, 'Booming Sector and De-Industrialization in a Small Open Economy', *The Economic Journal*, Vol. 92, No. 368, pp. 825–48.

Drysdale, P., 1988, *International Economic Pluralism: Economic Policy in East Asia and the Pacific*, Allen & Unwin, Sydney.

Drysdale, P. and Garnaut, R., 1993, 'The Pacific: An Application of a General Theory of Economic Integration' in C. Fred Bergsten and Marcus Nolan (eds), *Pacific Economic Dynamism and the International Economic System*, Institute of International Economics, Washington DC.

Economics References Committee, 2005, *Consenting Adults Deficits and Household Debt – Links between Australia's Current Account Deficit, the Demand for Imported Goods and Household Debt*, Senate Printing Unit, Parliament House, Canberra <www.aph.gov.au/Parliamentary_Business/Committees/Senate/Economics/Completed%20inquiries/2004-07/household_debt/index>.

Elek, A., 2009, 'APEC: Genesis and Challenges', in K. Kesavapany and Hank Lim (eds), *APEC at 20: Recall, Reflect, Remake*, Institute of Southeast Asian Studies, Singapore, pp. 1–14.

Emerson, C., 'Labor Is the Party of Competition', Speech to the Committee for Economic Development of Australia, 31 August 2009, Sydney <archive.innovation.gov.au/ministersarchive2010/emerson/Pages/LABORIS-THEPARTYOFCOMPETITION.html>.

Evans, G., 1992, 'Managing Policy and Organisational Change in the Department of Transport and Communications', *Canberra Bulletin of Public Administration*, No. 70, October.

Evans, G., 1995, 'Public Enterprise Reform in Australia', *Asian Review of Public Administration*, Vol. 7, No. 1, Jan–June.

Freebairn, J. and Corden, W.M., 2013, 'Vision Versus Prudence: Government Debt Financing of Investment', *Melbourne Institute Working Paper Series*, Working Paper No. 30/13, the University of Melbourne <www.melbourne-institute.com/miaesr/publications/working-paper-series/wps2013.html>.

Fukuyama, F., 1992, *The End of History and the Last Man*, Free Press, New York.

Fukuyama, F., 2012, 'The Future of History: Can Liberal Democracy Survive the Decline of the Middle Class?', *Foreign Affairs*, Vol. 91, No. 1 <www.foreignaffairs.com/articles/136782/francis-fukuyama/the-future-of-history>.

Garnaut, R., 1979, 'Australia's Shrinking Markets', in L.B. Krause and Sueo

Sekiguchi (eds), *Economic Interaction in the Pacific Basin*, Brookings Institution, Washington DC (also published in Japanese by the Japan Economic Research Centre, Tokyo).

Garnaut, R., 1989, *Australia and the Northeast Asian Ascendancy*, Australian Government Publishing Service, Canberra.

Garnaut, R., 1994a, 'Trade Liberalization and the Washington Consensus in Australia', in J. Williamson (ed.), *The Political Economy of Policy Reform*, Institute of International Economics, Washington DC, pp. 51–72.

Garnaut, R., 1994b, 'Open Regionalism: Its Analytic Basis and Relevance to the International System', *Journal of Asian Economics*, Vol. 5, No. 2, pp. 273–290.

Garnaut, R., 1996, *Open Regionalism & Trade Liberalization: An Asia Pacific Contribution to the World Trade System*, Institute of Southeast Asian Studies, Singapore.

Garnaut, R., 2001, *Social Democracy in Australia's Asian Future*, Asia Pacific Press, the Australian National University and Institute of Southeast Asian Studies, Singapore.

Garnaut, R., 2005a, 'Is Macroeconomics Dead? Monetary and Fiscal Policy in Historical Context', *Oxford Review of Economic Policy*, Vol. 21, No. 4, pp. 524–531.

Garnaut, R., 2005b, 'A New Open Regionalism in the Asia Pacific', in H. Soesastro and E. Pedrosa (eds), *The Future of APEC and Regionalism in Asia Pacific: Perspectives from the Second Track*, Centre for Strategic and International Studies (CSIS) and Pacific Economic Cooperation Council (PECC), pp. 108–129.

Garnaut, R., 2008, *The Garnaut Climate Change Review*, Cambridge University Press, Melbourne <www.garnautreview.org.au>.

Garnaut, R., 2011a, *The Garnaut Review 2011: Australia in the Global*

Response to Climate Change, Cambridge University Press, Melbourne <www.garnautreview.org.au>.

Garnaut, R., 2011b, *Garnaut Climate Change Review Update Paper 8: Transforming the Electricity Sector*, 29 March <www.garnautreview.org.au/update-2011/update-papers/up8-transforming-the-electricity-sector.html>.

Garnaut, R., 2012, 'Can Humanity Manage the Anthropocene: The Challenge of Climate Change', Address to the Annual Meeting of the Consortium of Humanities Centres and Institutes, Australian National University, Canberra, 15 June <www.rossgarnaut.com.au/Documents/Can%20Humanity%20Manage%20the%20Anthropocene%20Ross%20Garnaut%20150612v3.pdf>.

Garnaut, R., 2013a, 'Making the International System Work for the Platinum Age', in D.S. Prasada Rao and Bart van Ark (eds), *World Economic Performance: Past, Present and Future*, Edward Elgar Publishing, Cheltenham, UK, pp. 162–92.

Garnaut, R., 2013b, 'Monetary Policy and the Exchange Rate after Australia's China Resources Boom', PowerPoint presentation used in the 'Monetary Policy and the Exchange Rate for the End of the Resources Boom: Two Different Views' seminar with Peter Jonson at the Melbourne Institute of Applied Economic and Social Research, the University of Melbourne, 24 May <www.rossgarnaut.com.au/Documents/Monetary%20Policy%20Ross%20Garnaut%20Uni%20Melb%20240513v4.pdf>.

Garnaut, R., 2013c, 'Monetary and Exchange Rate Policy after the China Boom', PowerPoint presentation to the Committee of Economic Development of Australia, 18 July <www.ceda.com.au/media/324633/ccep072013_rgarnaut.pdf>.

Garnaut, R. and FitzGerald, V., 2002, *Review of Commonwealth-State Funding Final Report: A Review of the Allocation of Commonwealth Grants to the States and Territories*, Melbourne.

Garnaut, R. with Llewellyn-Smith, D., 2009, *The Great Crash of 2008*, Melbourne University Publishing, Melbourne.

Garnaut, R., Cai, F. and Song, L., 2013, *China: A New Model for Growth and Development*, Australian National University E-Press, Canberra, co-published with the Social Sciences Academic Press (China).

Gordon, R.J., 2012, 'Is U.S. Economic Growth Over? Faltering Innovation Confronts the Six Headwinds', *National Bureau of Economic Research Working Paper No. 18315* <www.nber.org/papers/w18315>.

Gregory, R.G., 1976, 'Some Implications of the Growth of the Mineral Sector', *Australian Journal of Agricultural Economics*, Vol. 20, Iss. 2, pp. 71–91.

Hewson, J. and Fischer, T., 1991, *Fightback!: The Liberal and National Parties' Plan to Rebuild and Reward Australia* (2 volumes), Liberal and National Parties, Canberra.

Hilmer, F.G., 1993, *National Competition Policy Report by the Independent Committee of Inquiry*, A. J. Law Commonwealth Government Printer, Canberra.

Hirsch, F., 1976, *Social Limits to Growth*, Harvard University Press, Cambridge.

Howard, J., 1999a, Reply to question without notice, Parliament House, Canberra, 28 September.

Howard, J., 1999b, Address at the 1999 Minerals Industry Dinner, Great Hall, Parliament House, Canberra, 2 June <pmtranscripts.dpmc.gov.au/browse.php?did=11360>.

Howard, J., 1999c, Address at the official opening of the Sir Roland Wilson Building, Australia National University, Canberra, 26 August <pmtranscripts.dpmc.gov.au/browse.php?did=11385>.

Howard, J., 1999d, Address to the Business Council Luncheon, Sydney, 17 June <pmtranscripts.dpmc.gov.au/browse.php?did=11336>.

Hyde, J., 2002, *Dry: In Defence of Economic Freedom. The Saga of How the Dries Changed the Australian Economy for the Better*, Institute of Public Affairs (Australia), Melbourne.

Intergovernmental Panel on Climate Change, 2013, *Climate Change 2013: The Physical Science Basis*, Fifth Assessment Report (AR5) <www.ipcc.ch/report/ar5/wg1/#.UlPheBCguSo>.

Kelly, P., 1992, *The End of Certainty: Power, Politics and Business in Australia*, Allen & Unwin, St Leonards.

Keynes, J.M., 2007 edition (first published 1936), *The General Theory of Employment, Interest and Money*, Palgrave Macmillan, New York.

Krugman, P., 1994, *The Age of Diminished Expectations: U.S. Economic Policy in the 1990s*, MIT Press, Cambridge MA.

Krugman, P., 2007, *The Conscience of a Liberal*, W.W. Norton and Company, New York.

Leigh, A., 2013, *Battlers and Billionaires: The Story of Inequality in Australia*, Black Inc., Melbourne.

MacFarlane, I., 1996, 'Making Monetary Policy: Perceptions and Reality', Paper presented to the Australian Economics Society's Twenty-Fifth Conference of Economists in Canberra <www.rba.gov.au/speeches/1996/sp-gov-250996.html>.

Machiavelli, N., 2002 (first published 1532), *The Prince*, translation by W.K. Marriott, the University of Adelaide, Adelaide <ebooks.adelaide.edu.au/m/machiavelli/niccolo/m149p>.

McLean, I., 2013, *Why Australia Prospered: The Shifting Sources of Economic Growth*, Princeton University Press, Princeton and Oxford.

Maddison, A., 2001, *The World Economy: A Millennial Report*, OECD Development Centre, Paris.

Marsh, I., 1995, *Beyond the Two Party System: Political Representation,*

Economic Competitiveness and Australian Politics, Cambridge University Press, Melbourne.

Martin, S., 1991, *A Pocket Full of Change: Banking and Deregulation: Conclusions and Recommendations of the House of Representatives Standing Committee on Finance and Public Administration*, Australian Government Publishing Service, Canberra.

Massachusetts Institute of Technology, 2011, *The Future of Natural Gas: An Interdisciplinary MIT Study* <mitei.mit.edu/publications/reports-studies/future-natural-gas>.

Meade, J.E., 1951, *The Balance of Payments*, Oxford University Press, London.

Painter, J., 2011, *Poles Apart: The International Reporting of Climate Scepticism*, University of Oxford, Reuters Institute for the Study of Journalism, Oxford.

Productivity Commission, 2013, *2013 PC Productivity Update*, <www.pc.gov.au/research/productivity/update/2013>.

Productivity Commission, 2013, *Electricity Network Regulatory Frameworks*, Report No. 62, Canberra.

Rattigan, G.A., 1986, *Industry Assistance: The Inside Story*, Melbourne University Press, Melbourne.

Rattigan, G.A. and Carmichael, W.B., 1996, *Trade Liberalisation: A Domestic Challenge for Industrial Nations*, National Centre for Development Studies, Australian National University, Canberra.

Reference Group on Welfare Reform, 2000, *Participation Support for a More Equitable Society: Final Report of the Reference Group on Welfare Reform*, Department of Family and Community Services, Canberra <pandora.nla.gov.au/pan/36764/20041216-0000/www.facs.gov.au/welfarereform/psmes2000/psmes2000.pdf>.

Richardson, S., 2013, the Foenander Lecture, 'Overworked and Underpaid?

The New Realities of the Labour Market' <fbe.unimelb.edu.au/alumni/events/alumni/recent_events/2013/foenander_lecture_2013>.

Sachs, J., 2012, *The Price of Civilisation: Virtue and Prosperity after the Economic Fall*, Vintage Books, London.

Schedvin, C.B., 1989, *Australia and the Great Depression*, Sydney University Press, Sydney.

Shann, E.O.G., 1927, *The Boom of 1890 – and Now: A Call to Australia to Put Her House in Order Lest Drought and Falling Prices for Wool and Wheat Overtake Us Again*, Cornstalk Publishing Company, Sydney.

Smith, A., 2011 (first published 1776), *The Wealth of Nations*, Simon & Brown.

Snape, R., 1977, 'Effects of Mineral Development and the Economy', *Australian Journal of Agricultural Economics*, Vol. 21, Iss. 3, pp. 147–56.

Spies-Butcher, B. and Wilson, S., 2008, 'Election 2007: Did the Union Campaign Succeed?', *Australian Review of Public Affairs* <www.australianreview.net/digest/2008/02/spies-butcher_wilson.html>.

Standing Committee on Infrastructure and Communications, 2013, *At What Cost? IT Pricing and the Australia Tax* <www.aph.gov.au/parliamentary_business/committees/house_of_representatives_committees?url=ic/itpricing/report.htm>.

Stiglitz, J.E., 2012, *The Price of Inequality: How Today's Divided Society Endangers Our Future*, W.W. Norton and Company, New York.

Wood, T., Hunter, A., O'Toole, M., Venkataraman, P. and Carter, L., 2012, *Putting the Customer Back in Front: How to Make Electricity Cheaper*, Grattan Institute <grattan.edu.au/publications/reports/post/putting-the-customer-back-in-front-how-to-make-electricity-prices-cheaper>.